IT Career: A Roadmap

Chukky Oparandu

Mondraim Books

A Mondraim Inc. Subsidiary

Also authored by Chukky Oparandu,

Mobile Phones and Tablets Repairs: A Complete Guide for Beginners and Professionals.

Available from Amazon.com, CreateSpace.com, and other retail outlets!

IT Career: A Roadmap

ISBN-13: 978-1533508850
ISBN-10: 1533508852

 Mondraim Books, a Mondraim Inc. subsidiary

Printed in the USA by Createspace

Available from Amazon.com, CreateSpace.com, and other retail outlets

Caution

Dedication

To Onyi, the love of my life – who holds so much promise for future technology; Iheoma my love, my pearl – inquisitive like daddy, sensitive like mummy; and my beloved Prince Chukwuma whose rule beckons – the majesty of my quiver!

Acknowledgments

I want to acknowledge the God of the universe who through the Holy Spirit inspired the writing and compilation of this work. The idea and motivation to keep going couldn't have come from anywhere else other than the divine.

First among mortals who provided the most valuable moral and material support is my beautiful and loving wife whose continual love and support is the fuel for my determination and strength; my chief critic, first assessor and the one who complements and completes me. Thank you for your patience living with one of the most difficult man on earth.

I appreciate my mother, Joy who brought me into this world, nurtured me and has continued to show understanding, checking up on my progress every once in a while; my sisters, Nkeiru – the rock, Amarachi, Chidinma and Akunna; and my only brother Nnanna for their continual moral support.

I am most grateful to Mr. Edmund Oparandu, who supported me during my early life's journeys and now, yet manages a crucial part of my business abroad. I value your contributions sir.

I cannot forget the support and motivation I got from everyone cited in the compilation of this work; who granted me permission to reference their works. I also appreciate my members of staff, Ms Jane my personal assistant; the staff of *Mondraim Inc.* and subsidiary *Mondraim Books* who debuted my first work, *Mobile Phones and Tablets Repairs: A Complete Guide for Beginners and Professionals* which has continued to help millions of youths across the globe. It has been a rare privilege working with you all.

And for every other person not mentioned but who played a part in the production of this work, I am very much grateful.

God bless you all.

Contents

Contents

FOUR

ICT Education and Training

FIVE

Starting and Building a Career in ICT

SIX

ICT: Visions for the Future

Preface

Information and Communication Technology is an industry comprising of a broad spectrum of relevant bodies of knowledge within foundationally established disciplines in Electronics, Computer Engineering, Computer science, and Telecommunication engineering. Therefore, an IT professional is an upwardly mobile practitioner in the industry who works formally or informally with a continuous currency of knowledge and skills to deliver value.

This book is not just about learning what ICT or ICT professionalism entails. It promises to enlighten a bit about ICT, but is more focused on enhancing a reader's mindset about what is; what is not and the roadmap to what possibilities exist towards achieving IT professionalism. This has become necessary because in my work as a coach, it has become too obvious that there exists an army of young people all over the world who have either passing or deep-seated interest in getting involved in the practice of ICT but are largely disillusioned by a lack of adequate guidance information; hence their confusion. Some are scantily engaged in activities they might tag as "IT" but lack an actual understanding of its structure, scale, and the big picture, thereby immersed in a vague pursuit that seem to lack either direction or a future.

The presence of innumerable ICT compliant devices in almost every sector of human endeavor might be stimulating this desire; most gadgets now feature digital computing and network connectivity capabilities, prime among which are digital mobile communication devices (e.g. smartphones, tablets).There is also a rising demand for IT professionals as invaluable human resources in organizations or as part of dedicated IT departments even as job losses are reported all over the world in other industry sectors. This rising demand can be attributed to the fact that most industrial machines and tools for business, trade, production and work routines of today leverage the sophistication, robustness, speed and accuracy; security and automation that computer hardware and software technology brings to the workplace. Therefore no matter the type or size of an organization, at one level or the other, there is a need for its business systems or operations to depend on Information and Communication Technology hardware or software infrastructures which in turn require capable trained personnel to both operate and administer.

This changing need of the workplace has led to the upwardly changing demand for skilled ICT labor; making many people, young and old to aspire to join the sector either as entry level workers, experienced hires with upscale skills or for private consultancy services.

However in most countries, the challenge has been in either an ICT knowledge deficiency or skill gaps among practitioners sufficient enough to meet international standards for successful project executions and industry growth or maturity. This deficiency in ICT knowledge amongst those already in the sector as well as new entrants has led to a shortsighted view on what "the big picture" of ICT entails. There seem to be a poor understanding about the connection that exists as a contiguous relationship from one knowledge area to another. This, more or less has contributed in some cases to poor image perception of the ICT profession; less confident ICT professionals with scant knowledge; and ICT project failures especially in third-world countries. The tertiary educational systems as well as most hiring industries are not to be left out of the blame as there has been a faulty focus and reliance on academic degrees from computer science disciplines alone, when talents could be sourced from a broader spectrum of disciplines.

All of the above stated concerns form part of the motivation from which the inspiration for this book is drawn. It is my view that talents for ICT practice or professionalism can be drawn from anywhere outside the core foundational disciplines of the ICT industry, provided the basic literacy needed for in-depth study and training exists. This is true because a great percentage of individuals especially in third world countries, commonly enroll into instructional institutions for disciplines they neither had inherent ability for nor hobby in prior to discovering at a later stage in life their purpose, talents, or interests. For such category of individuals, this book serves the purpose of enlightening them on the big picture perspective of pursuing a career in ICT as well as the pathway to achieve it.

The book ICT Roadmap therefore is not an instructional manual that teaches or equips you with the ICT skills and knowledge you need. Rather, it is a book that highlights, expounds, directs and guides you towards making that needed career decision earlier, armed with superior information. It is my hope that through this comprehensive overview on the ICT industry, a reader would appreciate very quickly the complete big picture perspective of ICT technology infrastructure, services, applications, inter-relationships, job roles and professionalism as well as the pathway to making an entry into the ICT industry with a higher level of certainty and confidence.

Life-camp, Abuja
Easter 2017

One

Introduction
To
The Specialty World of Information
And
Communication Technology

1

An Overview

Our world today contrasts very much from the world before now. Imagine there was a time when humans in different parts of the world thought that the world started and ended only around them. A time when man relied primarily on face to face meetings either on foot or on horsebacks to convey a message from one person to another if distance separates them; a time during the Middle Ages, when homing pigeons (messenger birds) were used to deliver short messages from any location within roughly a 400-mile radius to their home base. Pigeon post was alleged to be the world's fastest communication system throughout the Dark and Middle Ages, until around 1844 when Samuel Morse invented the telegraph while Guglielmo Marconi invented radio in 1895[1]. A time was, when communities broadcast messages using specially assigned community messengers who moved from street to street with a bell, announcing information for the general public. Then came the time of postal mail services; a time when important messages or information took days, weeks, months and even years to be accessed by other human recipients, during which period the validity, value or importance of the information may have become either obsolete, ineffective, unimportant, invalid or even lost its usefulness. A time was when information could only be described in terms of verbal communication in form of speech, conversation and later as text; a time information and communication existed solely between humans or at best between man and his beasts of burden or domestic pets.

Clearly, people of the medieval period were faced with several circumstantial limitations which hampered mobility, communications and communication media. Human populations were mostly cut off from each other during the Middle or Dark Ages. There was a gargantuan disconnect between peoples of different races, tribes, ethnic groups or nations dispersed across seas and oceans. For instance, literacy at that time was limited to one or two languages only, principally possessed by priests and the nobles thereby largely limiting the sharing of ideas to spoken words in the local language, making signs, gestures or the use of imagery. There was either no knowledge or scant knowledge of human existence elsewhere to each local community or nation not to speak of knowledge of the varieties of nature's resources and trade opportunities needed for survival. Such was the level of isolation at that time due to the limitations resulting from the absence of organized information and communication system and infrastructures.

What is Information?

One definition of information from dictionary is *"the act of informing or imparting knowledge; notification"*[2]. This means that information carries with it answers, and related in some way to knowledge or data.

Information represents a message, thought or any signal of value which takes one of several forms for expression through space conveying an intended meaning. Information therefore is usually defined in relation to its source – whether its existence is independent on it being observed or not, as either knowledge or data respectively. One can also deduce from this definition above that data and knowledge are regarded distinctly; data may be a derivative from information or parts of information as a resource, whereas knowledge is a derived quantity through cognitive observation.

Information parameters vary across systems from the natural to the unnatural; from human, animal or plant life to machines. For instance, information theory sees information as a sequence of alphabets which form an input that results into an output[3]; or as a type of input to an organism that results into an output in behavior or productivity, referred to as causal inputs by Dusenbery in his book *Sensory Ecology* [4]. Also it is seen as a

pattern that serves as an influence to transform other patterns and
so on.

However, regardless of what sense it is defined in, effort is
being made continually to harness, integrate and coordinate these
various forms of information into an intelligent dynamic world
system for the benefit of humanity.

The exchange of information between two disparate entities
through mutually understood signs, symbols, protocols or media
in order to convey intended meaning is what is known as
communication.

Technology refers to the sum total of systems, processes,
techniques or methods compositely designed to achieve a
purpose towards the production of goods or services.
Technology can also be defined as an in-built attribute embedded
in machines which are then operated by humans or as the skill
and knowledge acquired and applied towards the fulfillment of a
purpose – product or service.

When the technology deployed is towards the purpose of
achieving the transmission and reception of information from
source to destination and vice versa, it is then regarded as an
information and communication technology system.

Having understood what information, communication and
technology is, with focus on the information resource, it is easy
to notice that information in the early stages of man's
development on earth had a narrower meaning and application in
comparison to our world today. While there might be some kind
of similarities to the past in the various forms and ways man has
innovatively evolved information and communication systems,
yet it has broadened to include information from, to and for non-
living things (machines). Information and communication has
evolved to include that between man and machines; machine to
machine interactions; broadcast, multicast, and telecast
information and communication; voice, video, textual
information and communication; high speed instantaneous

information generation, transmission and reception for both short and long distances unimaginable in the past.

The discovery and advancement of science; and electrical, electronic and mechanical engineering technology has led to the dynamics, ubiquity and robustness of today's information and communication technology system. So important is information and communication that man has invested and continues to invest a greater percentage of the earth's resources in research; designing and building equipment and infrastructure for information gathering, interchange, exchange or communication at every level on earth and even outer space.

Our society exists primarily on social interactions and interdependency. Without communication from the basic family unit to nations of people, survival would have been difficult. Unless there exists a tool for interaction, collaboration, integration and cooperation such as an information and communication system, such things as knowledge sharing, shared bonds, shared values, shared goals, team work, synergy, shared existence with the capacity and ability to confront and defeat existential threats to humanity would have been a mirage.

As I write, the world has unanimously reacted to the use of chemical weapons in Syria against civilians in Syria's long fought civil war, culminating in a military response by the United States' president Donald J. Trump authorizing 59 Thomahawk missile strikes on a Syrian air force base[5]. This information, including the one about the use of chemical weapons with video evidence became viral across every part of the world in real time. One other thing is that this information became recorded and documented information worldwide in official, non-official, private and public archives on the information superhighway forever.

It is therefore for such necessity as these, that man has evolved through the ages to build an information and communication system that boasts gargantuan, expensive and robust technologies such as the various communication satellites launched into the earth's orbit and space; millions of kilometers of copper and fiber-optic cablings traversing the world, passing through marine habitats (the Atlantic, Mediterranean, Indian oceans) as well as terrestrial cable links traversing various countries and continents. There are also billions of cellular towers adorning the earth's skylines from city to city in every nation of the planet; billions of cellular and fixed wired or wireless telephone handsets; television satellites and cables; millions of network switches, routers and other communication network interconnectivity devices; billions of computers, servers and software; and a host of other devices that all aggregate together to form a huge internetwork (or the internet).

The extent to which mankind has succeeded in building information and communication system so far could not have been possible to achieve in isolation. Also, it has never been a once for all project where each unit of the overall system was accurately thought out, integrated and scaled to speed, size and efficiency at once. Rather it has been a gradual process although evolving differentially; it is streamlined, supervised, monitored and administered by international consortium of think-tanks, standards organizations and government who enact, implement and enforce regulatory policies and standards.

Some powerful bodies with such oversight responsibilities include the following;

A. The International Telecommunications Union (ITU) – is a specialized agency of the United Nations on ICT. Founded in Paris in 1865, it serves the field of information and communications technology. It is headquartered in Geneva, Switzerland with a membership of 193 countries, 700 private sector entities and academic institutions. Six official languages of ITU operation includes; English, French, Russia, Chinese, Arabic and Spanish. ITU allocates satellite orbits and radio spectrums globally as well as develops technical standards and policies for interconnecting networks and other technologies in telecommunication[6].

B. Electronic Industry Alliance (EIA) - This is also a standards and trade organization comprising an alliance of trade associations for electronics manufacturers in the United States. Their standards ensured that equipment of different manufacturers were compatible and interchangeable. The EIA ceased operations on February 11, 2011, but the former sectors continue to serve the constituencies of EIA[7].

C. International Organization for Standardization (ISO) – founded in 1947 with its headquarters in Geneva, Switzerland; English, French and Russia are its official languages, with a membership drawn from each of the national standards organizations of 163 countries. ISO's standards deal with a wide range of aspects of everyday life[8].

D. 3rd Generation Partnership Project 1 and 2 (3GPP1 and 3GPP2)

E. Organization for the Advancement of Structured Information Standards (OASIS)

F. Telecommunications Industry Association (TIA)

G. World Wide Web Consortium (W3C)

H. The International Electrotechnical Commission (IEC) – which creates and publishes standards for electrical and electronic technologies was founded in 1906, and headquartered in Geneva, Switzerland with 82 member countries. IEC standards used by countless electrical and electronic products manufacturers ensure that products work properly; connect to each other and operate safely[9].

I. Internet Engineering Task Force (IETF) – an open international community of network designers, operators, vendors, and researchers concerned with the evolution of the internet architecture as well as its smooth operation[10].

J. Global Standards Collaboration (GSC) – A senior level gathering of the world's leading information and communication technologies (ICT) standards organizations.

These are not all, as the list also includes regional and national bodies, sub-committees and agencies which have not been listed here. These organizations have helped create for us a new world; a world thriving successfully based on collaboration amongst individuals and corporate entities.

7

Machines and millions of devices which aid human communications are at the core of the sophistication and effectiveness of this collaboration. Just as humans learnt and leveraged the use of homing birds for communicating information in the middle ages, humans of today have also explored and tapped into the earth's rich resources to build devices that aid their communication processes. Human-to-machine and machine-to-human interactivity systems now control and coordinate the dynamics, speed and accuracy of this important aspect of living. We are living in the age of information! A world where billions of population of humans have become closer like one humongous global community of people who can share, communicate, care about one another, and conduct trade or business. We are living in an age of information driven by the combined technology trends of constantly-connected mobile communication devices and social networks, which have impacted the way we interact, live and do business.

For instance, an idea for a product can be formed in one remote locality in Africa, and initiated into actionable processes for production. Armed with technical inputs from different professionals located across several countries in Europe, America and Asia for different aspects of the design, the product would be developed. Using information and communication technologies like emails, phone calls, tele-presence conference calls, virtual private networks, web applications and platforms and so on, the sum total of information sharing, collaboration, financial transactions, product design and marketing can all be conducted without a physical meeting between all members of the team. Now, that is real power isn't it?

In our world today, we walk into shopping malls, offices and some homes with the doors automatically opening and closing after us due to sensory information input-output systems; Electronic key-cards with stored information ranging from code number passwords to biometric (fingerprint or iris scans) information provide security access control through doors. We also have artificial intelligence systems which improve or redefine human household experiences.

Less than six months ago, precisely on Monday, December 19 2016, Facebook CEO Mark Zuckerberg shared a video online about how he uses an artificial intelligence (AI) assistant he nicknamed Jarvis[11]. Jarvis is integrated to run his home security system and automate simple home-based tasks such as fetching a T-shirt from his wardrobe, making his favorite cup of tea in the kitchen, making a selection of his favorite music collection to play (probably depending on his mood, time of the day or any of several factors built into its algorithm), provide warnings when his baby wakes up from sleep, control lights, temperature, appliances and etcetera. The whole system was built to provide an experience similar to an invisible big brother that watches out for the needs of each member of the household in an intuitive, interactive, intelligent manner in real time. Wow!

Amazon created Alexa, an AI bot. Perhaps this press release by Accenture which was published by Techcrunch.com's Jonathan Shieber (@jshieber) on 12th April, 2017 would drive home what Artificial Intelligence means for our world today. It goes thus;

"With the rise of AI and voice recognition, customer experiences can be curated to the next level. Imagine Amazon's Alexa but with more emotion, depth and distinction. Accenture Interactive's PartyBOT is not simply a chatbot – It is equipped with the latest technologies in facial recognition that allow the bot to recognize user feelings through facial expressions, and words resulting in more meaningful conversations. Featured at this year's SXSW, the PartyBOT delivered an unparalleled party experience for our guests – detecting their preferences from favorite music, beverages and more. The PartyBOT went so far as to check in on every attending guest at the party, curating tailored activities based on their preferences. But the PartyBOT goes much further than facilitating great party experiences. Its machine learning applications can apply to range of industries from business to healthcare – acting as an agent to support patient recognition and diagnosis in hospitals that can recognize

*patient distress and seek the appropriate help from doctors. If
you would like to learn more about the PartyBOT, I'm happy to
put you in touch with our executives to discuss the applications
of our technology and potentially schedule time to see this in our
studios* "[12].

Pretty awesome, isn't it? A machine with emotions, able to
read and interpret human emotions as well! That's amazing stuff
you will agree with me.

The auto industry is not left out as information technology has
also redefined our transportation experience. Cars are becoming
more intuitive with in-built Geographic Information Systems
(GIS) that routes the driver to any desired location. We also have
self-driving cars like the ones by Google. Terrific features that
sense and auto-regulate room temperature through the air-
conditioning system, provide voice activated warnings to guide
against impact with other vehicles or objects and even
programmed self-parking capabilities into parking garages are
now common place!

A robust, transparent, secure and trustworthy information and
communication system of the 21st century has enabled seamless
financial transaction solutions and its management over-the-air
across space and time. Through social media networks and
internet portals; friendships, marriage, love, sex, healthcare,
religion, education and so on are either contacted, contracted or
conducted across races, cultures and nations. The divide has
been bridged. Whatever happens in one part of the world today
becomes common knowledge the world over through online or
TV news media round the clock, inducing shared emotional
response and impact on humanity.

Our world has changed and evolved in ways never before
imagined. The possibilities for the future with advances in
information technology are endless and awe-inspiring. We are at
the threshold of a period where information may be traded as a
raw resource, our environments becoming more attuned to
humans that it senses our presence, connects to and responds to
us. A period where big data is parsed for never before available

intelligence through artificial intelligence systems thereby helping in human decision-making; a period of multi-sensory communication where information will be absorbed through multiple dimensions of human senses; a time for human embedded chip technology – the possibility of having human-machine hybrids are even here with us!

How about Internet at the speed of thought? With embedded chips technology implant in humans, it will not be surprising to have human thoughts transmitted directly into the internet or from one human embedded chip to another. Now imagine walking down the street and without as much as saying an audible "Hi", someone just transmits "Hi" to other nearby human beings who are also carriers of embedded chips! Now that is getting scary isn't it? That will be a battle of human minds – mind power! Mind games! But wait for it. Here are a few technology innovations unveiled recently by Facebook. Facebook through her R&D lab, Building 8 revealed at F8 (Facebook Developer Conference, 2017) that it is working on a direct brain-computer interface that can allow users type texts just by thinking, without the need to first undergo surgical implantation of any chips! Rather, Facebook intends to optically scan the human user brain at the rate of 100 times per second to determine what the user is thinking or silently saying in his or her mind, then convert it to text. This way, the user types at 100 words per minute. That is, five times faster than typing on your phone this time using your brain! With this technology which is still in the early stages of development, it is Facebook's hope that it will power virtual/augmented reality. Then again, they unveiled another one called "skin-hearing". According to Facebook, sounds heard through the human ear's cochlea are converted into frequencies that the brain understands. Then, the skin which is covered in nerve endings converts physical sensations into ideas in the mind! And this has already been tested with some level of positive results – oops[13]! Clearly you can see where info-tech is heading!

The world is different today than ever before. It will never be the same again. Social networking, big data, constantly-connected mobile communication devices and cloud-based computing (cloud computing) are changing our life and business experiences in ways alien to mankind. Today, our world has become a community of digital citizens with perpetual connectivity to the world's information in our palms. With social media alone, humans have become very significant contributors to a large, continuously growing, robust, ubiquitous and intuitive information ecosystem far different from the world in ages past.

2

Defining the ICT (IT) Profession

Given the level of sophistication and complexity of the technologies deployed to achieve the purpose of operation and administration of the information and communication system; there must always be adequately trained, skilled knowledge workers manning a position at each layer of the ICT infrastructural system with well-defined specific responsibilities attached.

Therefore, making a career decision begins first from understanding the overall system architecture and framework, then aspiring to become a member of a specific professional group that forms part of the whole system. When you don't know where you are going, anywhere appears to be home until discomfort sets in!

Thus, ICT includes such practices as hardware and software systems building and design for a wide range of purposes either in a network or as stand-alone systems. Also inclusive are various kinds of information processing, structuring, and management; building intelligence into computer systems; multimedia systems and entertainment media; computer-aided scientific studies; information sourcing, acquisition and archival relevant to any specific purpose, and artificial intelligence systems. And of course, it is worthy to mention that ICT can assume other meanings as well, based on the context in which it is used given that almost all businesses, occupations and industry operations are being enabled by IT.

Information is the primary resource of value and interest. Therefore, it is important to keep in mind that information and communication technology (ICT) profession consists of practice within the ICT system revolving around the following aspects of the information cycle;

a. *Information Generation* - This entails the computation, formulation and composition of information from its various sources. Information constituents such as data, knowledge or any signal or input of value which expression must be given via communication from source to destination are generated in various ways. It could be generated from thought; from computation of variables or parameters; from natural or unnatural sources; from sound, light, electrical or mechanical sources; and from other innumerable kinds of visible and invisible matter.

b. *Information Capture or Acquisition* - This includes the methods and techniques by which information is acquired for analysis, processing, and storage.

c. *Information Analysis* which involves the process whereby information undergoes inspection and transformed into actionable knowledge. This is possible through information modeling, extracting value (knowledge) from raw data units through computation which is then applied towards decision-making.

d. *Information Processing* - includes but not limited to encoding, encryption, compression and packaging procedures and routines on information.

e. *Information Management* – refers to professional roles that involve the administration, control, and management of the information resource.

f. *Information Storage* – deals with the various ways and modes information is preserved such as digital, magnetic, optical, or holographic methods. Some service providers provide data warehousing services, virtualization or even cloud computing services. It is estimated that between the years 1986 to 2007, the world's technology capacity for information storage grew from 2.6 Exabyte (equivalent to 539 Megabytes of information per person) to 295 Exabyte (equivalent to about 44 Gigabytes of information per person)[14]. *The world's combined technological capacity to receive information through one-way broadcast networks was the informational equivalent of 174 newspapers per person per day in 2007*[15]. Imagine what it would have become in 2017!

g. *Information Security* – This consists of all professional services dealing with the protection of information from any kind of harm, tampering, damage or unauthorized access. It is the responsibility of professionals in such roles to ensure information integrity, safety, and privacy throughout its cycle from source to destination.

h. *Information Quality* - refers to the potential of the information to be free from any form of degradation due to distortions or interference. Information traffic congestions, as well as priority of communication issues can affect the speed of information delivery. The potential of a dataset to succeed in achieving definite practical or scientific objectives using assigned procedures for empirical analysis defines its quality.

i. *Information Presentation* - deals with visualization, display and other modes by which information is accessed, sent or received all through the information cycle.

j. *Information Infrastructure* - refers to the science, technology (hardware and software) and communication system that handles all aspects of the information cycle from source to destination and vice versa.

k. *Information Communication* - When we talk about information communication, we are actually referring to a merger of telecommunication, informatics, multimedia systems and its content and all other transmission and reception technologies.

<u>3</u>

Who is an ICT (IT) Professional?

An Information and Communication Technology (ICT) professional is one who *"Possesses a comprehensive and up-to-date understanding of a relevant body of knowledge; demonstrate on-going commitment to professional development via an appropriate combination of qualifications, certifications, work experience, non-formal and/or informal education; adhere to an agreed code of ethics/conduct and/or applicable regulatory practices and, through competent practice deliver value for stakeholders"*[16].

To be seen as, defined as, regarded as or embody the image of an IT personnel or practitioner, one must acquire a requisite composite knowledge and skill-set on a broad spectrum of specialty skills that form parts of the overall ICT system. As is common across numerous professions, there are basic knowledge and skills which neophytes in the profession must first be acquainted with. Sometimes, these are regarded as soft skills.

An IT professional must be conversant with the local, regional and international technical standards, policies and rules of practice in the field while keeping abreast with new knowledge and practice as technology advances. That someone is an expert today is not a guarantee that such person will remain so tomorrow if that person fails to update his or her knowledge and skills. Apart from the skills and tools of the trade, one must be knowledgeable about new products, their features, how they contribute to the information ecosystem and how they impact the lives of individuals and businesses.

A thoroughbred IT professional must be someone who understands how to merge, integrate or combine these products and technologies into value adding solutions for clientele. We are in the age of information driven by myriads of communication protocols of which the internet protocol, IP is chief. Products that are internet or web enabled are being rolled out almost daily. These products and tech-devices which are uniquely identified by their assigned device IDs and IP on the world-wide-web are owned and used by humans. Therefore, ownership of multiple address-able always-connected mobile and fixed home devices make the internet protocol numbering system a study every IT professional must know at the finger tips.

The importance and objective of the humongous communications system and infrastructures is to coordinate inter-relationships between every connected device (and by extension every connected human being), merging everyone and everything into one whole connected world system that is uniquely identifiable, track-able and reachable within nanoseconds. It is therefore the role of an IT professional to facilitate the efficient deployment of these technologies, transforming them into solutions. It is the professional who applies knowledge and skills to design systems that redefine individual user experiences, enhance and fortify business systems while making our world into one community of connected beings and things.

To summarize, the following basic attributes should serve to validate an IT professional's qualifications in order to be adjudged as deserving of the title;

a. He or she must acknowledge and be knowledgeable about the history and status of the ICT discipline.

b. He or she must be someone who thinks systemically by modeling organizations as a complex system within a complex environment; able to conduct comprehensive system analysis and implement the elements of a software development life cycle.

c. He or she must value ethics and its implications in professional practice by applying its basic theories; conform to professional integrity systems; establish what constitutes ICT ethical issues and apply ethical analysis methods.

d. He or she must be able to conduct requirements assessment by identifying, analyzing and interpreting every client's needs;

establish priorities, goals, constraints and uncertainties in a system.

e. He or she must possess and should be able to apply problem-solving skills, design and decision-making methods to create solutions for complex ICT problems.

f. A professional should be conversant with creating and implementing ICT design specifications that satisfy formal requirements such that it meets specified needs with appropriate consideration for public health and safety; and cultural, societal, and environmental considerations.

g. He or she must be capable of conducting rigorous testing of ICT systems to ensure compliance with user requirements and relevant extant policies and standards.

h. He or she should be innovative and able to synthesize alternative solutions from concepts and alternative procedures.

i. He or she must demonstrate information skills, critical and analytical thinking as well as the ability to carry out researches.

j. His or her communication and coordination skills must be to a high proficiency level in listening, reading, speaking, and writing English for professional practice.

k. Finally but not conclusively, he or she must demonstrate relevant expertise; able to function independently, validate competence in ICT operations and continuously obtain and retain updated appropriate IT certifications.

These IT skills and knowledge-area attributes listed above are common to all ICT professions covering ethics and professionalism, problem-solving skills, interpersonal communications, design, abstraction and modeling.

It is therefore remarkably apparent that there is a depth and complexity far removed from the scant, perceptual knowledge on the streets especially in most third-world countries that tends to narrow information and communication technology to computers (repairs, maintenance or desktop computing), software programming and web design or development. No, it goes far beyond that with multiple skill-levels and specialty areas we shall examine during the course of this book, which presents a huge opportunity for entry for anyone who is interested. It is like a buffet; make your pick and run with it.

While the objective of this book is to expose the opportunities and pathways of entry into the industry for anyone, it is important to point out that there are actually slight limitations to ICT practice in some specialties if someone is not well versed in any one of the core foundational disciplines. However, there is a plethora of standalone courses and certifications which an outsider to the ICT field's foundational disciplines may undertake to attain certain skill levels in order to operate within specific IT roles. By the time one might have gone through this book, it is my belief that he or she should be able to make an informed decision on which career path to follow; at what skill or job level to enter or exit; to what level of expertise one may set his or her goals; and finally what kind of education or coursework to pursue.

Two

Information
And
Communication Technology Discipline

<u>4</u>

The Dictates of Disciplines

A discipline is a subject area, field of study or branch of learning devoted towards expounding knowledge and transferring skills for practice. It is usually difficult to define Information and Communication Technology as a discipline considering the numerous established disciplines from which it is drawn and which independently can lay claim as ICT disciplines as well. For instance, Intel and a host of other chip-making companies in Silicon Valley, USA are regarded as IT companies in some quarters. But the art, science, research and skills involved in the making of an electronic semi-conductor chip comes primarily from the knowledge, skills and practice of electrical, mechanical (thermodynamics, metallurgy) and electronic engineering disciplines among others. It therefore seems like the end-user industries for which the products of these microchip-making companies are serving often determine their classification as ICT companies by the media and most people.

But identifying and making this observation however, does not in any way make such a classification as erroneous, false or inappropriate; it is indeed true based on context that they belong to the ICT category. What it means is that categorization of information and communication technology knowledge area in the 21st century into a core discipline may not be that simplistic except for one to descriptively accept it as a discipline of disciplines. ICT is such a discipline that, by virtue of what represents value and meaning to the society today, has given purpose and meaning to the existence and practice of its 'parent' disciplines. Those 'parent' disciplines, from which ICT is derived, now exist primarily to serve the purpose and existence of their 'offspring-discipline', thereby deriving meaning from it - (i.e. ICT). The preceding root-knowledge ('parent disciplines') become meaningful and relevant only if and when they are used or deployed towards creating value and solutions that satisfy the requirements, policies, protocols, theories and practice of information and communication technology.

It should not be surprising therefore, to find that the overshadowing discipline in the workplace of today that coordinates and manages the activities of core-discipline engineers at the back-end are likely to be ICT knowledgeable geeks. IT's complexity and challenges with its hybrid infrastructure, composite applications and services; changing growth or development approaches, workplace mobility issues, speed of service delivery; end-users and IT staff's experience as well as a constantly increasing amount of data all contribute to this possibility. Only professionals trained specifically to place these requirements and challenges in perspective rather than be distracted with core engineering design issues are saddled with such responsibilities.

Typically, a student earns a bachelor's degree as an entry-level qualification, preparatory to a career in ICT in any one of these main computing disciplines;

- Computer engineering
- Computer Science
- Software engineering
- Telecommunications Engineering (with Networking)
- Information Technology (Not common and recent)
- Information Systems (Not common and recent)

Because ICT provides such a broad range of choices, it is impracticable for anyone to turn out to be proficient in all of its knowledge areas. Consequently, anyone who wishes to become an ICT professional as I stated earlier requires a specific focus for his or her professional life.

<u>5</u>

Foundational Root Bodies of Knowledge for ICT

Foundational root bodies of knowledge for ICT refer to the amalgam of erstwhile root disciplines which formed the basis for the growth, development and synthesis of the new knowledge area known as ICT. The sciences, engineering and mathematics branches of knowledge are foundational to the birth of modern computing hence, information and communication technology. Each branch of root knowledge developed from one to another all through the ages as knowledge was being organized into various disciplines to cater to diverse professions.

Whereas science deals with measurable or systematic principles and knowledge derived from scientific methods, mathematics deals with abstract representational systems employed for studying numbers, shapes, structures, change as well as the relationships between these concepts while engineering on the other hand deals with the application of both science and mathematics to provide solutions to human problems.

The specific core (root) bodies of knowledge within these root branches of knowledge include the following;

Science

Science, by definition and based on my initial premise that each root discipline developed from one to another, is broad and could be regarded as the "mother" root of the technological and engineering knowledge tree. Take a look below.

Science is categorized into;
a. *Natural Sciences* – This is further sub-categorized into *Physical science* and *Life science*. Physical science subjects or courses include physics, chemistry, earth sciences, and space science. Under life sciences we have biology.

b. Social Sciences – The social sciences include subjects or courses like psychology, sociology, criminology, archeology, anthropology, human geography, pedagogy, international relations, political science, law and linguistics.

c. Formal Sciences – This is further sub-categorized into mathematics, systems theory, statistics, logic, decisions theory, and theoretical computer sciences branches of learning.

d. Applied Sciences – Engineering and Healthcare are key branches of knowledge under applied sciences. Under engineering, we have core disciplines like agricultural, biomedical, computer, civil, chemical, electrical, electronics, industrial, genetic, mechanical, mining, military, nuclear, robotics, and software engineering disciplines. While healthcare disciplines include medicine, veterinary, dentistry, midwifery, epidemiology, pharmacy and nursing. Computer science is also an applied science discipline.

There are also interdisciplinary courses or subject areas which cut across branches and sub-branches of learning.

Engineering

From the science 'mother-root' and applied sciences 'daughter-root' above, we find that engineering disciplines which influence information and communication technology knowledge areas originated. But among the broad sub-categories of engineering disciplines are a 'select few' of which their impacts on ICT are highest. As a student or graduate whose interest is in the pursuit of ICT professionalism, undergoing academic studies in any of the science or engineering disciplines provides you with the base foundation knowledge common for all entrants into these branches of knowledge. But closest to ICT in terms of knowledge-depth, commonality and 'family-tie' are the following engineering disciplines;

Electrical Engineering: Electrical engineering is a branch of engineering that deals with the study, technology and applications of electricity and its associated concepts. This field branched out to other fields including electrical power systems generation and transmission, electronics, control systems, electrical instrumentation, telecommunication, radio-frequency engineering, signal processing, microelectronics and computer engineering. Electrical engineers are therefore versatile and adapt easily to changing and emerging technologies as well its application.

Electronic Engineering: As seen above, knowledge continues to evolve; one branch giving birth to another. Electronics is the main sub-category out of a combination of physics and electrical engineering that gave birth to computer, radio frequency (RF) systems engineering, telecommunications, remote sensing, digital circuits, instrumentation, optoelectronics and microelectronics. Others are signal processing, embedded systems, audio, video and broadcast engineering.

The relationship between electrical and electronics engineering is reinforced by the fact that most universities and institutions of higher learning combine both as a taught course of study in schools. The job sectors that mainly employ electrical and electronics engineers are national and state governments, research and development industries, manufacturing industries and engineering services companies.

Telecommunications Engineering: The use of radio frequencies, wire, any of the various electromagnetic systems or optics to transmit signals, messages, signs, sounds, images or any other form of information from one place to another is the focus of telecommunication engineering. It is one of the closest to ICT and involves the use and application of multiple technologies. Networking or network engineering is a part of this course.

Computer Engineering: Computer engineering synthesizes knowledge from electrical and electronics engineering with computer science and mathematics. Concepts such as circuit design, circuit analysis and synthesis help in understanding computer systems and systems integration which are common practices in computer engineering for developing computer hardware and software systems.

Training in electronic engineering is required in addition to hardware–software integration. This is needed for design of microcontrollers, microprocessors, personal computers and super computers. Embedded microcontroller technologies, software and firmware coding, mixed-signal circuit board designs and operating system development all fall within the job details and competencies expected of students of this discipline. It has both strong and close affinity as a foundational course and part of the ICT discipline. Also the current trends and adoption of robotics, artificial intelligence (AI) innovative technologies have their roots in computer engineering as specialty areas. It is the student's decision ultimately, to specialize. Other courses include computational science and engineering; computer networks, mobile computing and distributed systems; coding, cryptography and information protection; computer systems architecture and parallel processing etcetera.

Software Engineering: Applying engineering principles and procedures or methodology to software design and development is what software engineering entails. It is far more than just writing software codes. IEEE standard glossary of software terminology defines software engineering as *"the application of a systematic, disciplined, quantifiable approach to the development, operation and maintenance of software"*[1]. Software engineering is a narrower, more definitive, software-focused specialty than computer science with such sub-disciplines or subject areas as requirements engineering, software design, software maintenance, software testing, software construction, software development process, software configuration management, software quality, and software engineering economics. A good number of universities worldwide offer Bachelor of Software Engineering programs; Masters-level and doctorate-level programs including certificate courses are also available.

Computer Science: Computer science is another relevant foundational discipline for ICT. Because of its broad-based coverage of abstraction, modeling and the computing tasks native to computers, it has the closest affinity to information and communication technology.

Whereas software engineering has its native root and draws a lot of principles from computer engineering, computer science integrates mathematical logic and computation to software engineering knowledge and methodologies. Software engineering is focused on more than just writing software to developing systematically, in line with sound engineering practices, quality software that meets specifications, delivered on time within budget through a rigorous, measurable process. Computer science on the other hand focuses on the theories, science and practical approach to computation. The way and manner information is acquired, represented, accessed, processed, communicated or stored is of interest to computer science; hence it tries to build algorithms that automate these processes.

As a pointer to this, some of its subject areas include; theory of computation, algorithms and data structures, theory of programming languages, information and coding theory. Others are computer performance analysis, computational science, human-computer interaction, databases, then computer graphics and visualization. It also shares studies in similar areas with computer engineering or software engineering like in artificial intelligence, computer architecture and engineering, computer networks, computer security and cryptography as well as software engineering. These shared courses are usually just a speck of knowledge different in depth of content from when pursuing those disciplines as major.

Mathematics: Mathematics is a branch of formal science that uses abstract representational systems to study numbers, shapes, structures, changes, space as well as the relationships existing between them to derive meaning. Mathematics observes patterns, makes computations, draw inferences from them to determine the truth or falsity of assumptions or conjectures. Abstraction and logic are fully in the domain of mathematics and employed fully in computer science; but not just that, mathematics is required in all the natural and applied sciences especially in engineering. Mathematics is a universal language to the sciences. Galileo Galilei (1564 – 1642) said;

"Philosophy is written in that great book which ever lies before our eyes — I mean the universe — but we cannot understand it if we do not first learn the language and grasp the symbols, in which it is written. This book is written in the mathematical language, and the symbols are triangles, circles and other geometrical figures, without whose help it is impossible to comprehend a single word of it; without which one wanders in vain through a dark labyrinth."[2]

It was from applied mathematics other disciplines like statistics, game theory, logic and even theoretical computer science evolved from. The relationship and foundational link to ICT can also be seen in how most schools combine computer science and mathematics as a taught program in the universities.

From the foregoing narrative on the foundational disciplines for ICT, analyzing from what I refer to as the sciences 'mother-root' branch of learning, it is clear that having a science background from secondary or high school education to tertiary levels would play a major role in the ability of any interested candidate into ICT to scale in depth and grasp, leading to great heights of competencies faster. However, we cannot presume expressly that someone whose academic pursuits have primarily been based in the non-science disciplines up to tertiary levels can neither cope nor acquire ICT knowledge and skills relevant to professional practice. On the contrary, it is possible to make such a switch and that is part of the thrust of this book; to help in bringing clarity to both the right foundation paths and also optional paths towards ICT professionalism.

For instance, there was a report by *Australia's Digital Pulse* in 2015 on a statistics conducted by *Deloitte Access Economics* in partnership with Australian Computer Society (ACS), that 43% of ICT workers in Australia studied courses other than ICT or engineering! Imagine that! If you extend that statistical survey to most countries around the world, I bet you it may be the same or even a higher percentage especially in 'third-world' developing countries. Another observation was that *"52% of ICT workers are in industries outside ICT itself, including professional services, public administration and financial services"* [3].

However, industry-specific and vendor-specific ICT certification programs provided by professional bodies and mainstream IT vendors respectively are helping to bridge the gap between traditional entry requirements to ICT and current realities within the ICT industries.

Also, a look at the foundational disciplines and schools' academic curricula shows that core knowledge areas most times are not streamlined to current realities of ICT professional role requirements. Most of them are wide-ranging although the basic background knowledge to get you started in the industry might be covered in slight depths in some, in greater depths in others and scantily in others. It is therefore the responsibility of intending professionals or students to make their pick according to the closest in affinity to the area of ICT professionalism sought after; then, address specialty or role-specific needs with additional training workshops, certifications, or short certificate courses.

For aspiring young people to ICT professionalism; ready-for-college or university students, it must be clear at this point where you should be headed in pursuit of further education as a first step. For undergraduates who are already in any of the academic faculties among the foundational root disciplines; those who want to digitize their professions or enter the ICT industry from other professions as well as those already in ICT but need clearer visions, the next sections ahead will provide you with improved clarity on ICT career paths and competence requirements.

<u>6</u>

Foundational ICT Bodies of Knowledge

In spite of the foundational root bodies of knowledge for ICT discipline's evolution, there are core bodies of knowledge that address specifically the ICT discipline's knowledge areas suited for practice in the field. Over the years, the professional landscape of ICT practice can best be described as fragmented. This may possibly be due to a combination of the vast breadth of knowledge involved; the knowledge overlaps and knowledge gaps which define IT from its foundational root disciplines.

Attempts to streamline the practice across various national professional bodies, regulatory authorities, industry stakeholders and certifying vendors were being made only in recent years. For instance, according to a report for the European Commission in 2012 on '*e-Skills and ICT Professionalism: Fostering the ICT profession in Europe*'[4], they concluded that in order to foster the growth of digital jobs in Europe and to improve ICT professionalism, there needed to be a '*Framework for ICT Professionalism*'. Then, they decided and proposed that the framework would comprise the following four building blocks or pillars for an ICT profession;

    i.   *A Body of Knowledge*
    ii. *A Competence Framework*
    iii. *Education and Training*
    iv. *A Code of Professional Ethics* [5]

Therefore, having a common method of referencing standard ICT knowledge as is the case with other professional disciplines, will provide a solid reference library that gauges and validates professional competence, certification programs and examinations, academic taught programs as well as industry human resource development initiatives.

Having learnt so far about the root knowledge disciplines that preceded ICT practice disciplines, it is essential for aspiring professionals to know and understand the foundational ICT bodies of knowledge as duly identified. It is primarily a compendium of the common base knowledge which is required as a reference point for entry into the practice of ICT.

Using the list provided by the *European Foundational ICT Body of Knowledge* as a baseline, we shall examine in short details a classification of knowledge areas which ICT professionals must understand at entry. Twelve knowledge areas are identified. They include;

- *ICT Strategy & Governance*
- *ICT Business and Market*
- *ICT Project Management*
- *ICT Security Management*
- *ICT Quality Management*
- *ICT Architecture*
- *Data and Information Management*
- *Network and Systems Integration*
- *Software Design and Development*
- *Human-Computer Interaction*
- *Software Testing*
- *ICT Operations Management.* [6]

The list no doubt is very comprehensive. Remember that the primary objective of ICT body of knowledge is to define the building blocks of all the knowledge areas in the ICT field. Subsequently, it then acts as a guide for professionals to understand the scope of ICT knowledge required.

Every discipline has foundational bodies of knowledge or knowledge areas that define its existence. Take for instance the root foundational bodies of knowledge for ICT earlier discussed. A discipline like Software Engineering has a Software

Engineering Body of Knowledge (SWEBOK, 2004) compiled by the IEEE Computer Society which defines ten software engineering knowledge areas that are further broken down into 251 topics[7]. And it has its own root from other bodies of knowledge while being one of ICT's root foundational bodies of knowledge! So in working towards finding a common body of knowledge for ICT, great effort went into research, collaboration, brainstorming and input from all stakeholders in ICT, other bodies of knowledge, complimentary disciplines and internationally established frameworks to arrive at an acceptable document.

This is important because ICT has become an all encompassing, invaluable and inextricable enabler of systems, communications, value and operations in business and our daily lives. The latest trend about *'pervasive computing'*[8] which objective is to integrate computing ability into every product bring this reality closer. ICT therefore cuts across multiple fields and disciplines.

The ICT foundational body of knowledge elements are further categorized and grouped to make it easier to match or adapt them into job roles or profiles. The categorization actually relates to the methods and building blocks developed from knowledge overlaps across the vast breadth of knowledge areas in the ICT field.

The 12 above-listed ICT foundational bodies of knowledge are broken into two categories. They are *ICT Professional Knowledge* and *ICT Problem-solving Knowledge* areas[9]. These two classifications form the core of six ICT foundational bodies of knowledge building blocks. The remaining blocks are grouped appropriately under each of these two. They are *Technology Building, Technology Resources, ICT Services Management and ICT Outcomes Management*[10].

ICT Professional Knowledge Areas
It must be obvious at this point that the ICT foundational body of knowledge area one chooses has a nexus with the expected job

profiles of aspiring or practicing ICT professionals. Also, competencies in ICT follow an expertise skill-level structure rated from bottom to top, entry-level to master. However, certain professional competencies are better learned through professional growth across multiple levels and stages in the profession starting from the entry point. It is in such cases that the phrase, "experience is the best teacher" proves true while others are achieved through studies or direct training.

ICT professionalism covers a wide range of issues which addresses job performance in the industry expected of any practitioner. "ICT Professional knowledge" areas identified are the following;

- *Ethics*
- *Professionalism*
- *Teamwork concepts and issues*
- *Interpersonal communication*
- *Societal issues/Legal issues/Privacy*
- *History of ICT discipline* [11]

These are knowledge dimensions that are cross-cutting and apply to each of the 12 foundational Knowledge Areas listed above. Every aspiring professional entering the ICT domain will have to gain insight into these aspects during the course of education and training.

Ethics deals with ICT-specific professional integrity systems, methods and processes of ethical analysis, professional attitudes and behaviors while *professionalism* addresses concepts such as accountability, responsibility, expertise, certification, competence, excellence, reflection, and self-government in practice.

Teamwork concepts and issues concerns group dynamics, leadership, collaboration, conflict resolution, and developing teams while *interpersonal communication* revolve around the ability for writing technical reports, making oral and written presentations, writing user documentations and developing effective interpersonal skills. It also includes skills that complement job-specific skills in order to enhance personal relationships in the workplace, job performance and job prospects.

Societal issues relates to privacy and civil rights; social freedoms, computer fraud, intellectual property and legal issues while the *history of ICT discipline* is meant to help professionals gain knowledge of the evolution sequence and process of the ICT discipline from inception as well as keep abreast of the currency of happenings within the industry.

ICT Problem-solving Knowledge Areas
ICT professionalism has its primary focus on solutions. Incidentally, the kinds of problems which require an ICT professional's technical input are usually abstracts (intangible). Unlike other professions like medicine for example where you have a human body; engineering, you have buildings – that is, tangible things. ICT deals with abstract concepts that can neither be touched nor felt. The computing disciplines form a huge part of ICT professionalism and is concerned with using abstraction methods and modeling tools to understand problems, design solutions and handle abstraction. Therefore, the other four building blocks of the ICT foundational bodies of knowledge are grouped under this core category.

Technology Building consists of such knowledge areas as Software Design and Development, Human-Computer Interaction; Information system lifecycle services beginning from system analysis to design, construction and software testing.

Technology Resources includes bodies of knowledge in ICT Architecture, Data and Information Management as well as Network and Systems Integration.

ICT Services Management building block consists of knowledge bodies such as ICT Project Management, ICT Security Management, ICT Quality Management and ICT Operations Management.

33

ICT Outcomes Management building block has ICT Strategy and Governance and ICT Business and Market classified under it.

In the next section, we shall be looking at the summary details of what each of these foundational bodies of knowledge are and how they map into the usually advertised job profiles seen in job vacancy advertisements.

<u>7</u>

Matching Foundational ICT Bodies of Knowledge to Job Profiles

The workplace of the 21st century is ICT driven. Any small, medium or large-scale enterprise that must thrive in the information driven marketplace of today must embrace IT. Business productivity is driven primarily by information technology connectivity solutions for operational efficiency. This is because businesses survive on intra-business and inter-business communications which improves collaboration, reduction in costs of doing business and information sharing leading to greater yields and value.,

However, it is instructive to note that across professional job roles, distinguishing knowledge gaps between disciplines continues to narrow. What seems to be of utmost relevance and importance to 21st century industries is the ability to transfer skills and knowledge across multiple professional job roles. This attribute is known as "versatility". It is no longer enough to just be a technical expert with knowledge of one specific ICT domain. ICT has grown from just being a back office tool or department in an organization to become a key strategic asset in everyday professional life, permeating through every organizational unit and layer. So the ICT industry is looking for professionals with multi-disciplinary skills who also have good understanding of business and technology. An instance of this is when one's computer science knowledge and skills can be utilized to solve engineering problems, logistics issues or management challenges. To be easily employable and stay competitive, a professional must be capable of combining specialization in one specific ICT domain with a breadth of relevant ICT knowledge.

In order to understand the requirements of various advertised ICT job roles or titles in the industry today – and they are quite numerous, with similar job profiles titled differently by different organizations - thereby making a choice of the right fit that matches one's specific IT skills, let us examine a match between standardized ICT foundational bodies of knowledge and their associated job profiles, roles or titles and expected responsibilities.

ICT Outcomes Management Building Block

ICT Outcomes Management knowledge area is concerned with roles that empower the professional to understand the big picture perspective of the impact, benefit and advantage of consuming or deploying ICT resources in a business or organization. It evaluates roles critical in managing and implementing change within various organizations; the integration of ICT roles into business units which objective is to leverage ICT tools and infrastructure to gain a competitive edge. Below are the foundational bodies of knowledge which outlines the common features that should correspond with industry nomenclature role titles adopted by any organization.

ICT Strategy and Governance

Every organization or business is setup with specific goals and objectives. It may or may not be engaged in the pursuit of economic benefits. However every organizational system determines one way or the other if her activities lead to the achievement of individual or corporate value. Business value proposition therefore is of utmost importance when considering ICT strategic investments in the systems, methods and processes that formulates, implement and achieve it. This is where ICT strategy and governance roles become relevant.

In order to derive maximum value from ICT investments, any business or organization must be entrepreneurial in approach. In his book, *Innovation and Entrepreneurship,* Peter Drucker suggests that *"entrepreneurship is not a personality trait of an individual or entity"*. Rather, he suggests that entrepreneurship is a characteristic; a *"behavior"* exhibited through practice by an individual or an entity. In the same book, he stated that *"innovation is the specific tool"* which entrepreneurs should use to take advantage of *"change"*; therefore see change as an *"opportunity"* to engage in a different business or service[12].

What this means is that given the dynamics and speed of business change, an understanding of how the information systems can be managed to the utmost advantage of an organization is a key factor for every business or organization to be innovative in the 21st century in order to deliver value. ICT strategy and governance roles must therefore be assigned to professionals who understand how information systems augment business operations; that understands and can explain information management processes; and understands how to innovatively administer, control and allocate business resources to areas of higher productivity and better results using a sound business strategy.

ICT governance systematically cuts across every organizational unit from the board of directors to executive management, staff, customers, communities, regulators and investors. It identifies and establishes connections to systems that help in achieving the potentials in ICT for business success. IT governance also relates to managing organizational issues using governance principles that shape the conduct of IT business, especially as regards moral behavior. These governance principles guide the conscience of the professionals in meeting their core mandates. IT governance professionals address organizational issues such as business change management, culture issues and race relations.

The job profiles or roles usually assigned to people with this competence are; ICT Consultant, Chief Information Officer (CIO), Business Information Manager (BIM), Business Analyst, Chief Technology Officer (CTO) and other equivalent titles.

Professionals of this cadre are expected to possess certifications such as COBIT, Six Sigma, Lean, ISO 38500, and CGEIT (Certified in the governance of Enterprise IT) among other vendor-specific ones. However, if you are eyeing plum positions like this, understand that its requirements go along with years of experience especially in IT management roles. Despite whatever background discipline you possess already, an MBA (Masters in Business Management) will be an advantage as complementary knowledge to ICT. Skills in domains such as business process improvement, enterprise and business architecture development; business risk management, sustainability strategy, innovation and research; business change management and so on are required. So it is a senior management leadership position in which the business operational processes, policies, strategy, and plans are determined; then integrated into the overall ICT infrastructure investments. ICT is then used to drive the business towards greater efficiency and profitability.

In this era of "big data", "social media", "cloud computing" and "pervasive computing" devices, a business needs ICT and governance professionals to possess the ability to quickly identify, recognize and leverage *"change"*; especially because changing business dynamics, trends and sometimes big unexpected occurrences could make or mar a business. As Peter Drucker said, *"innovation is a specific tool"* needed to leverage change *"as an opportunity"* to change the direction of the business[13]. Therefore time and speed are vital in recognizing when "change" is taking place from the enormous data pool at a business' disposal. That is where business analytics using big data tools are of essence.

Years ago, Bill Gates – Microsoft's Co-founder – in his book *Business @ The Speed Of Thought* recounted a story which exemplifies the impact of late response to changing trends on a business. He said, *"We didn't see that the internet, a network of academics and techies would blossom into the global commercial network it is today"*. Talk about a disruptive phenomenon! Then he said, *"The internet's sudden growth in popularity changed all the rules"*! And what was the result of this oversight; this inability to quickly identify and respond to "changing" trends? Hear him, "in *fact, in 1995 various experts predicted that the internet would put Microsoft out of business. This was bad news on a colossal scale. We used our digital nervous system to respond to that crisis."*[14] Good a thing he knew that it was a business crisis! I could risk a guess if he were to write another book and decides to share about the arrival of mobile computing (the smartphone and Android OS revolution); we might read a similar tale.

Finally, if you aspire to drive and be responsible for ICT strategy and governance in any organization, you should be knowledgeable enough and prepared to lead and grow the business; otherwise the business' ICT investments will be wasted.

ICT Business and Market

While ICT strategy and governance oversees the business with the perspective of ways ICT is integrated into business strategy and policies, ICT Business and Market roles take a more granular look at ICT itself; what ICT business entails. It is roles that evaluate and articulate ICT's role, value and business transactions within the system. It looks at the various ways ICT interacts with the business unit. Such concepts as supply chain management, ICT business "insourcing"; outsourcing; "nearshoring"; "offshoring"; and "homeshoring" are involved.

Businesses need competent professionals who are capable of determining, managing and controlling - in line with the prevailing business' ICT strategy – the most suitable in-house ICT business model and market for business efficiency. Take for instance the concept of insourcing whereby in-house employees are pooled together to handle a process or to produce or develop a needed software product otherwise handled by third-party outsourcing firms or vendors. The decision-making processes required on whether to in-source or outsource an ICT service or business and the relevant market components involved can only be made by a competent professional who understands these concepts and their impacts (merits or demerits) very well.

Industry nomenclature role titles such as Supply Chain Manager, Project Manager, Enterprise Architect and Account Manager are usually common titles associated with this knowledge area. Others which are a match as well are Business Information Manager, Business Analyst; ICT Infrastructure Manager and ICT Consultant titles. Some organizations may even tag it a "Head of IT"/xxx where "xxx" is a specific business unit within the organization. This time let's analyze a real world job advert just for further insight. Below is a sample job advert for a Business Analyst position;

Leading investment firm looking to appoint a degreed, analytically strong Business Analyst with 2-4 years experience;

Description: *Analyze, design, test and implement business requirements and processes.*

Main Responsibilities: *With an ever growing client base, we are looking for someone who will be able to <u>understand</u> the diverse <u>needs</u> of our internal users, <u>assess</u> the impact of proposed solutions, <u>capture</u>, <u>analyze</u> and <u>document</u> <u>requirements</u> (within an agile environment) and then <u>support</u> the communication and delivery of those requirements. The team is very passionate in creating <u>efficiency</u> by <u>automating</u> workflow and leveraging of our backend systems, so the candidate is expected to be passionate about creating efficiency and redesigning business processes.*

Key Attributes of the Role
Problem-solving and Solution Design
- *Strong analytical and <u>problem-solving skills</u> including a thorough <u>understanding</u> of how to interpret business*

needs and translate them into application and operational requirements.

- *Able to critically evaluate information gathered from multiple sources, reconcile conflicts, decompose high level information into details, abstract up from low level information to a general understanding and distinguish user requests from the underlying true needs.*

Requirements Elicitation

- *Able to identify key stakeholders and gather requirements for specific problems/opportunities.*
- *Elicit requirements using a range of techniques.*
- *Able to drive and challenge business areas on their assumption in an effort to come up with solid solutions.*

Value Identification

- *Able to recognize and articulate the expected customer value for a specific problem.*
- *Able to use the knowledge of our internal (and potential external) systems to maximize business value.*

Presentation and Facilitation

- *Excellent verbal and written communication skills and the ability to interact professionally with a diverse group including executives, managers and subject matter experts.*
- *Able to prepare and present content as well as facilitate workshops. Able to drive agreement and outcomes even when there are conflicting views/stakeholders.*

Communication and Listening

- *Be the liaison between the business units, IT domains and your team members.*
- *Able to actively listen, be responsive and express thoughts effectively*

Documentation and Written Communication

- *Develop requirements specifications to an appropriate level of detail, using various techniques while conforming to team standards.*

- *Able to <u>interpret</u> and express the needs of our users through visuals e.g. mock-ups and user journeys*

Project Management and Implementation

- *Able to <u>plan</u> and <u>manage</u> individual projects whilst coordinating stakeholders and timelines*
- *Able to <u>support</u> and drive the implementations*
- *Minimum Qualifications*

Relevant tertiary qualification (e.g. Information Systems, Software Development, Systems/Data Analysis, Bachelor of Communication, Bachelor of Business Science) with strong academic performance

2 years' experience in web technologies

5 years' experience in a business analysis role

2 years' experience in financial services sector

Skills/Competences and Experience

Experience in the use of <u>business analysis</u> frameworks and methodologies; Also familiarity with agile <u>software development</u> practices, SQL skills and <u>databases knowledge</u>.

Wow! A very comprehensive and detailed enumeration of what type of candidate this company is seeking. The underlined words are by this author. Can you see the correlation with everything we have been discussing so far? Always take keen note of keywords used when reading through job requirements documents – especially re-occurring keywords. Do you also notice the cross-functional feature of the Business Analyst title among the foundational bodies of knowledge? I believe you do. There is even a bit of project management skills required in this case.

As you will discover when we discuss "ICT Education and Training" in chapter four, it is not enough to just write and pass the exams to earn a certificate as many are guilty of this. When you qualify in knowledge, skills and experience for a position, you will 'know'. Reading through job requirements in vacancy advertisements, it will be easier to make the right choice that fits your profile. Part of this book's objective for already practicing professionals is to help remove personal doubts and confusions about real capabilities – and for real, it is possible to sometimes have needless self doubts; then, for those yet to get into the industry, to be definite about the type and quality of education to pursue in order to arrive at desired career destination.

ICT Services Management Building Block
Service management is concerned with activities that involve the daily operational routines an organization or business unit engages in, which encompasses the structure of communications; processes and interactions between the Business's ICT personnel and business customers or end users.

ICT service management roles are responsible for the efficient management of the day-to-day operational activities between the IT service desk team (technical personnel) and the business or end-user customers.

ICT service managers combine knowledge of business with their ability to build and support the ICT technology infrastructure to scale seamlessly. The relevant foundational bodies of knowledge that make up this building block; ICT Project management, Security management, Quality management; and Operations management are discussed below.

ICT Project Management
A business or organization may either be a start- up on its ICT investment journey as a totally new project from inception; an existing firm trying to integrate ICT into their already non-ICT driven operations; or an ICT compliant firm with supplementary ongoing ICT projects often initiated according to diverse needs. Whichever is the category, ICT solutions to short-term and long-term problems that often arise in an organization will always give rise to ICT projects. And this is part of IT service management – managing ICT services - to the organization.

The totality of hardware and software tools, equipment and systems represent the information and communication technology infrastructure of an organization. While numerous individual technical expertise and skills often work together to put the entire system in place, the effectiveness, efficiency and benefits of the system is impossible without proper management of man and materials. Project managers are therefore professional business managers who are capable of making effective and efficient project management decisions, sometimes through the support of appropriate project management software; integrating specific project management knowledge and techniques with understanding of business. Their primary objective is the successful execution of IT development projects from planning to execution.

Project Managers decompose a problem using modeling; analyze and decide on strategies; and weigh options based on available data using technical or non-technical tools which aid them in creating a project plan. Such other knowledge they have to acquire and apply is in the area of risk management, people management and a thorough understanding of processes and procedures. They also require knowledge in, but not limited to change management; costing; cost-benefit analysis; econometrics fundamentals; financial management; project reporting and presentation methods; and scheduling.

In the industry, such position titles as Chief Information Officer (CIO), IT Project Manager, and ICT Operations Manager are common nomenclature. Among others, common certifications include PRINCE2® Foundation and Practitioner (i.e. Projects IN Controlled Environments); IPMA certifications i.e. (International Project Management Association); Project Management Institute's certifications (PMP, CAMP, PgMP, PfMP, PMI-ACP, PMI-PBA, PMI-RMP, and PMI-SP) and other vendor-specific IT certifications.

ICT Security Management
When you talk ICT or IT security, it includes all human, hardware and software security configurations and access control built into IT systems infrastructure to regulate, control and protect the integrity, privacy and availability of data.

However, security and access control must align with the business strategy and goals in order not to become a source of administrative bottleneck to critical, seamless flow of information to desired business units as and when necessary. If it is not properly managed, security may slow or limit the responsiveness of the information system during mission-critical situations.

IT security managers must therefore strike a balance between strictly prohibitive security policy implementations and overall administrative or business policies.

Like all management roles, IT security management professionals must possess adequate understanding of business. The basic interacting units and elements of every business or organization consists of the board; management; employees; product and services development unit; customer care and business customers; partners; finance and accounts; order processing; marketing and sales. Whether the organization is a commercial or non-commercial entity, all or a few exceptions out of the above-listed are critical parts of the system. Therefore, maintaining the relationships, flow and security of data among these units in a safe and effective manner is a big challenge to IT security.

In the book, *Managing by Wire: Using IT to Transform a Business* by Steve H. Haeckel and Richard L. Nolan, they stated that *"A firm's IQ is determined by the degree to which its IT infrastructure connects, shares and structure information; Isolated applications and data no matter how impressive can produce idiot savants but not a highly functional corporate behavior"*[15]. It is an obvious requirement therefore, that security planning and management must be streamlined with the project management team's goal of creating a ubiquitous, connected and structured information system that encourages knowledge sharing.

The job titles commonly associated with this ICT foundational knowledge area are ICT Security Manager, Systems

Administrator, ICT Security Specialist, and ICT Operations Manager.

Some recommended non-vendor certifications include; ISACA's CISM (Certified Information Security Management, CISA (Certified Information Systems Auditor), CISSP (Certified Information Systems Security Professional), ISM (Information Security Management – ITILv3, CREST (Council of Registered Ethical Security Testers) and EnCASE (a proprietary guidance software designed for forensics, cyber security, security analytics and e-discovery). ISACA is Information Systems Audit and Control Association. Visit http://www.isaca.org for more information.

In summary, ICT security management therefore encompasses management of computer system security, physical security, procedural security, communication security and software security by IT personnel, equipment vendors and end-users.

ICT Quality Management
ICT quality management deals with the overall quality rating of applications and infrastructure used in the business. The goal of IT quality management is to ensure business value is improved in general. It monitors and evaluates the entire processes leading to the acquisition of hardware and software infrastructure; the quality of staff involved; the type and quality of vendors procured from and agreements reached; the quality of skills deployed by staff involved in implementation, support and maintenance of the applications and hardware – including computer systems and network devices; the specifications and requirements; quality assurance and audit.

The quality of the business infrastructure and human resource determines the level of value derived from the business by all stakeholders. It is therefore necessary that someone oversees the system with the eye of a hawk with the sole responsibility of ensuring that quality is not compromised with quantity. Undermining quality is undermining the integrity of the whole system.

In the industry, equivalent position titles for this knowledge area are as Quality Assurance Manager, ICT Operations Manager or ICT Service Manager.

International Standards Organization's certification for process quality, ISO9001, ISO/IEC Information Technology (Process assessment option) certification, Capability Maturity Model (CMM) certifications and CMMI for Instructor, Practitioner and Appraiser categories.

ICT Operations Management

The word 'operation' denotes *"the methods or practice by which a device performs its functions"*[16]. But in the sense of an information system, 'operations' management has more significant connotations.

All through our discussions on other knowledge areas within this same ICT Service Management building block, you would observe that the industry position title of "ICT Operations Manager" cuts across virtually all the others. Consequently, it points to the significance of this knowledge base which deals with operational details; the effective, smooth, uninterrupted daily functioning of the hardware, software applications and the human resource operations staff.

While "ICT Strategy and Governance" conceptualizes and creates business strategies, "Project Management" creates actionable designs that together with "IT Security Management" ensure efficient, smooth, seamless interactions between the business units; then, "ICT Operations Management" maintains and provides continuous technical support for the working blueprint of the ICT infrastructure, ensuring it does not fail. "ICT Quality Management" maintains a hawk-eyed oversight on "ICT Operations" to enforce strict adherence to standards that are in line with organizational policies and meet agreed service levels in their duties.

Industry nomenclature ICT role titles include Service Manager; Project Manager; ICT Operations Manager; Service Desk Agent; Network Specialist; Technology Specialist; Key Account

Manager. In some cases, the prefix "ICT" or "IT" may come before the titles listed, among other equivalent titles.

Relevant certifications include; ITIL and COBIT among other vendor-specific certifications.

Technology Building "Building Block"
Technology building "building block" of the ICT foundational bodies of knowledge considers professional roles focused on the building of technology capacity to run the information system. Professional roles that facilitate hardware and software acquisitions; software development; hardware integration; as well as the human resource capacity to develop useful, usable applications using several programming languages are grouped under this building block.

The information system lifecycle usually depends on such knowledge and skills as requirement analysis, design, construction, testing, operation and maintenance, in that order. It is a systematic lifecycle which requires adequate knowledge of the methods and processes of system development.

Hardware is important and crucial; just as the body is to the spirit, so also hardware to software. But the intelligence behind the information system is usually resident in the software technology that runs on various hardware platforms. Similar to biology, hardware is like the human anatomical and skeletal system comprising of every interconnecting bones, ligaments, tissues, organs and so on. The digital information system has its soul, mind and intellect residing mainly in the software running on the system's hardware infrastructure.

It is however pertinent to note that software does not eliminate the human factor in making strategic business decisions. What the software technology does is to tremendously aid the decision-making process across board for all knowledge workers.

Therefore, "ICT Technology Building" knowledge areas focus on defining those professional bodies of knowledge specialized towards building software or integrating hardware to achieve the strategic business objectives of an organization. The ICT foundational knowledge areas classified under this building block includes software design and development, human-computer interaction and software testing.

Software Design and Development

A software system can be regarded as an information system; an information system, as a software system. This does not preclude the fact that the backbone is the hardware infrastructure. The intangible key concept, "information" has almost – if not – all its elements in software; the data, its capture or acquisition, analysis, processing and so on.

The software system which serves to handle these information processing and analysis is designed and developed by applying sound engineering principles and practices in order for it to meet end-user requirements and satisfy business goals.

Software design and development professionals must therefore be knowledgeable in system development lifecycles, programming languages, object-oriented programming, user interface design, software architecture, requirements engineering and system integration. These were core course units I took during my Master's degree program in Information Technology. However I believe if you are aspiring to specialize in this knowledge area, studies should begin from first degree in the relevant computing or root-foundational ICT disciplines discussed earlier. Postgraduate education alone is rarely enough to major in developing complex business software.

Some of the common industry position titles for professionals with this knowledge area are Systems Architect; Software Developer; Test Specialist; IT Systems Analyst; Systems Administrator; Network Specialist among other equivalent titles.

Besides recommended academic degrees in relevant disciplines, there are also certifications available from industry vendors which we shall be discussing in chapter 4 "ICT Education and Training". Others are CompTIA (Computing Technology Industry and Association), IEEE's Certified

Software Development Professional certification, Open Group's Certified IT Specialist, and ASL (Application Services Library).

Human-Computer Interaction

The Association for Computing Machinery (ACM) defines Human–computer interaction (HCI) as *"a discipline concerned with the design, evaluation and implementation of interactive computing systems for human use and with the study of major phenomena surrounding them"*[17].

This knowledge area focuses on developing frameworks for user-centric design considerations in building applications and the information system. User interface technologies and human-machine interaction systems are more prevalent today than any time in the history of mankind. Therefore, keeping in view the human user in IT applications and systems development is very essential all through the system development lifecycle.

Knowledge areas include ergonomics, cognitive psychology, user interface design, accessibility standards and user-centered design methods.

Corresponding industry role titles for this foundational knowledge area include System Architect; Testing Specialist; Software or Systems Developer; and Digital Media Specialist among other related titles.

Relevant certifications are similar to those recommended for Software Design and Development.

Software Testing

Before someone can test or investigate the usefulness; assess the usability or otherwise; the technical compliance to accepted standards and regulations of a software product, such a person must either be a competent user or a competent design engineer.

Software testing professionals are required to investigate and make available, reports to relevant stakeholders about the quality of a software product or service and provide information by which an objective assessment would help appraise possible benefits and risks associated with using software.

Software testing also includes finding and fixing software bugs, beta testing, line by line code execution and software lifecycle testing. The job profiles in the industry matched to this knowledge area are no different from that of software design and development foundational body of knowledge. Therefore, software testing professionals' role titles include software developer title, software test specialist, system administrator, digital media specialist and so on.

Technology Resources Building Block

A resource according to wiktionary refers to *"something that one uses to achieve an objective e.g. raw materials or personnel"*[18]. Therefore, when that "something" is a technology, it then means that the qualifier, "technology" is added before the word, "resource".

Technology resources are those components of an information and communication technology system which give support to the system to achieve its purpose. They include the software systems, the hardware infrastructure and the personnel that supports and operate the information system.

Therefore, the ICT foundational bodies of knowledge found under this building block outlines the knowledge and skills which demonstrate adequate understanding of computer hardware and software; the frameworks of ICT architecture; data and information management resources; and network resources.

Let us examine the knowledge areas below.

ICT Architecture

High level knowledge in Computer systems architecture; business architecture; data architecture; applications architecture; technical architecture; and enterprise architecture are the focus of this foundational body of knowledge in ICT.

The entire business strategy, business solutions design, and the information and communication system of a firm function based on frameworks with built-in details to the smallest unit. Without business architecture, business chain of command and communication would make no meaning; without solution architecture, there would be little basis on which business problems would be solved; and if the information system has no structural design (architecture), its sustainability is impossible.

The business scale, corporate traditions and structure altogether determine the kind and nature of execution required for any one of these architectures. Therefore intelligent consideration is given to these factors for every implementation to succeed.

Common industry titles include IT Architect; Business Architect; System Architect; Solutions Architect; Enterprise Architect; and System Analyst. It is not uncommon to find these specialized knowledge professionals working alongside IT Project Managers or ICT Consultants. An aspiring professional to these roles must have IT backgrounds in related fields with growth experience from the bottom up for there to be high, positive performance impact.

The relevant certifications rated for these roles which are recommended are usually at the peak level of vendor certification tracks. For instance, a Cisco Certified Internetwork Expert (CCIE), Cisco Certified Design Expert (CCDE) or Cisco Certified Architect (CCAr) certification qualifies one to assume the role of any of the architect titles provided the candidate must have grown through some years of active service in the industry in related capacities down the ladder. There is also The Business Architects Association and other bodies that offer certifications.

Data and Information Management

Data management involves every act, policy, or control measures put in place for the effective administration and protection of the integrity and confidentiality of data and information.

As part of the "Technology Resources" building block of ICT foundational bodies of knowledge, data and information management knowledge is essential because "data" and "information" are the core resources of an information system – hence, a business or organization – around which every other technology resource revolves. Without them the business architecture, enterprise architecture and almost every other architecture and objective would literally be baseless.

The knowledge base required covers the learning of such competencies as data capture methodologies, data modeling, data organization and structuring; also data storage and retrieval, database management systems, data conversions and processing, data encoding and encryption techniques; document, records and content management.

Equivalent industry role titles corresponding to professionals with this knowledge area are; Business Information Manager; Database Administrator; System Administrator; Systems Architect; and Software Developer or simply "Developer". Also, Network Specialists and Test Specialists possess the knowledge background for such cross-cutting roles.

To qualify for this knowledge area, it is recommended to undertake similar educational and certification programs as enumerated for those cross-cutting role titles identified. Vendor-specific certification education would suffice too. Examples include Oracle, Microsoft certifications or even the Software Engineering Institute's programs.

Network and Systems Integration

Throughout this section, we have talked about various crucial bodies of knowledge for developing management capacities that bring about positive business outcomes through ICT; first, by creating ICT strategies and governance principles; then utilizing the knowledge and skills focused on the business and market of ICT for achieving organizational or business goals.

We have also understood knowledge areas that focus on managing the continuous servicing of the information system; from project management initiation and planning through quality of service, security and then to operational sustainability.

Then, we also explored those foundational bodies of knowledge responsible for preparing the ICT professional to build the kind of technology systems that fully meets the requirements of the business, stakeholders and end-users or business customers; making sure that the system deployed does not carry with it risks that are inimical to users or conflicts with relevant regulations, business policies or cultural inclinations.

Finally, we arrived at the granular core theme on which all the other knowledge areas lean; the resource of concern and focus; of value – data and information. We have seen how through different categories of systems' architecture or structural design, the "big picture" perspective's framework is translated into an integrated functional entity; the focal elements of information and data managed and manipulated within it.

However, the practical integration of the activities of these interrelated and interacting frameworks and technology resources (human, information, data and so on) cannot be complete without the vital role of network communication technology resources. Network and systems integration knowledge is very essential - and of high industry demand- for designing and implementing the computer system networks on which organizations depend on to connect, share and archive information. Adequate knowledge in networking fundamentals (concepts and protocols, switching, routing, building and optimizing scalable networks, Local Area Networks, Wide Area Networks, Metropolitan Area Networks, and Wireless Networking); data communication; interconnecting disparate software applications and systems; and Software-Defined Networking (SDN) are necessary to achieve this.

The breadth of knowledge and skills network and system integrators cover is enormous. Other subject areas include Network architecture; Network components and operating systems; Wireless and mobile computing; and Distributed systems. Others are Voice over Internet Protocol (VoIP); System infrastructure dimensioning; Middleware; Programming; Telecommunication systems; and Web technology.

Despite covering the generic knowledge and technology base for networking and system integration, much more is required to earn a position in most cases. The industry is replete with various competing original equipment manufacturers (OEM) and vendors' categories of networking gears and products. Therefore, it is necessary to gain "multi-vendor-specific" knowledge to be versatile and valuable in the industry. We shall discuss this in detail in subsequent chapters.

The common job role titles in the industry matched to this body of knowledge are Network Engineer, Network Specialist, System Engineer, ICT Consultant, and Digital Media Specialist, Network Architect and other equivalent titles.

One common trend about top-level ICT foundational knowledge areas is management capacity. For any technology specialty in Engineering or ICT to be complete, leading to career growth into "middle-management" or "senior management" roles in any organization, the aspiring professional must also acquire academic or professional certifications in management in addition to the possession of some years of experience in relevant IT roles. Technical specialization is just simply not enough, especially to lead!

However, most comprehensive ICT academic core curriculum in higher institutions offering ICT-specific disciplines usually include to a sufficient degree, taught IT management courses. For some, management courses are only available in postgraduate Master's and doctorate degree programs.

Also, understand that besides technical and managerial competences found within the foundational bodies of knowledge which are largely categorized under "ICT Problem-solving Knowledge" area, one major criteria for hiring ICT professionals in real life is a demonstration of an equal possession of "Professional Knowledge" area skills. Both are necessary. Majority of "Professional Knowledge" skills relate to a possession of what is referred to as "emotional intelligence competencies". This is very important especially if you need to assume leadership positions.

Daniel Goleman, an authority in emotional intelligence studied 181 different positions in 121 different companies and organizations and analyzed a list of required competencies needed for top performance in a given job, role or field. In his book, *"Working with Emotional Intelligence"* he stated his findings which was based on classifying those competencies according to whether they were cognitive skills, technical skills or emotional competence skills. One among many other positions he studied was for information technology project managers. And after analyzing a list of several key competencies essential for top performance as IT Project Managers in a particular company, he discovered that 73 percent of the abilities were emotional intelligence abilities. He concluded that, the higher percentage of emotional competence abilities as a requirement for top performance in job roles, held true at about 67 percent when he carried out the analysis on the rest of the 181 different positions. "[19].

It is therefore of immense importance that a leading ICT manager possesses soft skills such as people skills, high achievement drive, influence, self awareness and political awareness; he should have empathy, initiative and be able to function independently among other interpersonal and communication skills.

"The labor of the foolish wearies every one of them, because he knows not how to go to the city"

~ **Ecclesiastes 10:15** (Holy Bible, KJV)

Three

Understanding

The

ICT Industry and Practice

<u>8</u>

Questions about IT Jobs and Practice

Fresh out of schools' academic and practical trainings or industry certification programs, some exigent concerns that typically occupy the minds of successful aspiring professionals include such questions as;

- Where does one find that first ICT job; where is the ICT industry found; or what kinds of firms typify a sector in the ICT industry?
- What are the available options for a career in ICT? In what ways is ICT best practiced?
- What type of organization or corporation will provide either the best latitude or the best platform or both, for practicing someone's skills; for professional career growth and increase in learning or experience?

The foregoing questions or more – depending on personal career dispositions – symbolizes some few valid concerns most professionals enthusiastic about excellence in any particular field of practice experience. There may be more decision-factors of concern; for instance, for some the level of compensation may rank highest on their list of priorities.

The ubiquitous nature of ICT today – as seen in the simplest business task or routine of every private, public or corporate entity - makes it appropriate to define the ICT industry as a global corporate industry and is found in every private, public or corporate business entity. It could be as significantly modest as that small business powered with one or more internet-enabled smartphones.

Therefore, regardless of the ICT compliance ratings – the level of adoption of ICT in a business – every small business entity possesses all of the basic elements of every business. It may be just one "employee" (Owner-manager) who has "customers" that receive ("delivery") "products and services" in exchange for money ("revenue"); with inherent business "costs" and business "competitors". While there might seem to be no formal structure or defined business process, the tools for achieving successful business operations - its informal information systems - constitute part of the global information and communication system.

For example, at its most fundamental levels, a business handles customer order requests via a phone call, a web application or a direct customer walk-in. The transaction process involved in any one of these three modes of order processing would result eventually into the generation, capture, storage and retrieval of one or more kinds of data. How? One may wonder, particularly in the case of a walk-in customer transaction. At the very least, the business' sales record (for a product) of the item sold must be documented somehow, somewhere or someday. If it was a service, without even a slight trace of information concerning the transaction documented, the fact is that there is always a direct or indirect correlation between numbers that tell the full story. An income entry for instance, signifies a product sold, a service charge earned, an inventory data (stock reduced), a delivery data, a re-tooling or re-stocking issue and so on. Summarily, every transaction affects data in one way or the other, directly or indirectly. Consequently, there exists in every business entity- private, public or corporate – the potential opportunity for the intervention of ICT for effectiveness, efficiency and higher productivity.

What this means is that, to a large extent beyond the traditional professional growth system (which is equally very important, anyway), the acquisition and possession of a bouquet of ICT bodies of knowledge, competence or skills is a call for "out-of-box" thinking; innovativeness, initiative, creativity and solution-provider disposition all the way through.

Professional career growth is not largely dependent on any ICT organization or firm one works in. It does contribute to it. But professional career growth and development depends largely on individual responsibility; each professional determining personal growth by the diligent pursuit and acquisition of desired relevant and update professional knowledge and skills. This is achieved through consistent studies, training programs or seminars; industry and vendor-specific certification programs or academic degree programs. This is possible – including career experience – through employment within corporate ICT compliant firms or while actively engaged in 'Private' IT consulting practice. On this, we shall be discussing in details – pros, cons and recommendations in Chapter 6 (Building a Career in ICT).

Whether a consciously determined choice is made or circumstances (providence) thrust it upon anyone to either work in corporate ICT organizations or engage in Private IT practice, the focus should be on how it provides the latitude and platform for one to apply those skills for the benefit of mankind. When service to humanity becomes the consuming passion of a professional, professional growth; increased knowledge or professional experience; and improved financial benefits become guaranteed.

To understand the industry better, we shall be examining in details, the four core segments of ICT industry practice in the next sections. They are; ICT consulting, ICT service providers, ICT OEMs and vendors and ICT Consumer (ICT compliant) organizations.

2

ICT Consulting Organizations

A 'consult' means *to seek opinion or advice; to deliberate on; to seek out a solution*[1]. In the context of ICT consultancy, it refers to working as a consultant or contractor rather than as a full time employee in a firm, whereby a professional offers IT advisory services.

The act of "consultation" hereby establishes an existence of a relationship between two disproportionate individuals or entities on a specific issue at hand; the inequality factor largely dependent on a knowledge or skill resource possessed by one and needed by the other.

ICT consulting organizations are workforce repositories of the ICT human resource, focused primarily on the provision of ICT problem-solving solutions. They provide IT advisory on the best possible ways a business can leverage IT to achieve her business objectives such as business strategy and design; implementation; deployment; administration or provision of outsourced service management services at premium service charges.

ICT consulting organizations are to a large extent "bespoke" ICT solution providers. Bespoke because in most cases they adapt custom-made solutions for different clients (individuals or corporate entities) based on established requirements from the problem statements made during the consultation process. The difference between ICT Consulting organizations and "ICT Service Providers" is that although "consulting" is also part of their activities, ICT Service Providers usually own and control the ICT service infrastructure, the terms of service, and the specifications available for a service. Therefore, in most cases their "service" is generic and designed for all business customers while ICT consulting firms leverage their (ICT Service Providers) products and services in their own service to the customer; for whom they tailor solutions according to their needs, mutually agreed terms, service levels, specifications and scope.

The strength, reputation and client base of an ICT consulting organization are determined by the quality of her human resource responsible primarily for ICT advisory services and project implementation.

An ICT Consulting organization's service focus differs from one firm to another. One firm may focus on just one type of ICT service while another may focus on two or more clusters of ICT services.

Any service area which is the focus of an ICT Consulting firm determines the IT skill-set they would seek after for their staffing needs; and is also related to the ICT foundational bodies of knowledge we examined earlier, especially the specialization areas. Evaluating a firm's activities is helpful in deciding if an organization is suitable for providing one's skills with enough latitude and platform to thrive or not.

One advantage of working in a mono-service or multi-services ICT consulting organization is the inherent opportunities it presents, working on a variety of challenging customer issues. An active firm with consistent, varied and voluminous client-base is the best place to start out growing your IT skills. Unless one is interested only in a monotonous routine job with a steady pay check, I would recommend a place to first nurture, learn and grow your IT skill set. If the alternative is to be changing jobs from time to time in line with a goal to tap from the service focus of different organizations over a period, the better and faster one's overall career growth will be.

The size of an ICT consulting organization varies; from one staff (the experienced, highly skilled ICT professional business owner and one branch office) to thousands of employees and branches nationwide or worldwide. This literally means that one person can actually represent an "ICT Consulting Organization" once that person sets up a practice!

Therefore, depending on the level of saturation or drought in the IT skills market, compensation levels differ and for a higher percentage of workplaces, it is not very fabulous comparatively for certain skill sets and skill levels. However, this is not in any way an indication that ICT practice does not enjoy exciting benefits packages. On the contrary, it is among the highest earning professional industry currently. ICT firms usually get adequate compensations for contracts executed and in-high-demand skill sets also enjoy excellent remunerations. This is because there are specific industry averages for each country or region of the world. "Standards" practicing companies respect such demands.

However, the problem is in the disparities across different companies; in their management dispositions to staff welfare;

their revenue base and company size which may play a role in under-compensation. A small company may handle big contracts, earn huge revenues yet low on staff compensation. It is a two edged sword anyway. Adequate staff compensation and benefits attracts and retains the right quality of staff for meeting the demands of high paying clientele and vice versa. But if as a professional, you know your worth in the industry yet you are not well compensated, it is recommended that you continue to work earnestly; patiently learning before considering a next move. Money is not everything although it is very important for motivation and well-being.

Some of the systems by which IT consulting organizations or firms operates are;

- As self employed contractors or consultants. This can be as a privately owned limited liability firm or in-house, off-shore, or near-shore employees of IT firms on contract agreements and arrangement.
- As IT Professional services organization providing "mono-focused" or multilateral ICT services with a large pool of IT workforce.
- As IT consulting organization focused on providing temporary or long term contractual staffing requirements for businesses in need of specific IT skills from time to time. This helps to augment shortages of skilled personnel on short term projects or to fill in urgent, interim sometimes unexpected staff absences.
- As IT subject matter specialists on lease as consultants to organizations that require external, third-party opinions and recommendations on short-term special skills ICT projects. This is common especially with advancements in technology. Sometimes it is not always financially convenient for organizations to hire and retain certain categories of high value IT personnel on a permanent payroll.
- As ICT consulting organization that takes total control of a part or whole of the IT services of a client.

- As ICT security consultants. Security is a special need and special skill area that is in most cases outsourced to ICT Consulting organizations. IT security consultants may be self employed professionals managing a number of business portfolios.

Before we wrap up this section, let us see a summary example list of services ICT Consulting organizations engage in;

i. IT managed services solutions (part or whole)
ii. ICT project sizing and planning
iii. Designing business processes
iv. Designing business systems
v. Project management support
vi. Network design and implementation
vii. Specific technology features implementation, tuning, optimization and monitoring
viii. Infrastructure capacity planning
ix. IT staffing (Technical Talent Recruitment/Placement)

10

ICT Service Provider Organizations

ICT Service Provider organizations primarily satisfy one, two or three of the "IT Service Management" goals of any business or client organization. What are these service management goals? They are classified into three, namely;

- Internal service
- External service
- Shared service

By virtue of the foregoing classification, IT Service Provider Organizations are thereby categorized as either Internal Service Providers; External Service Providers or Shared Service Providers.

As pointed out in the previous section, although a Service provider may own and control the specifications and terms of service of the IT infrastructure, they can still offer "consulting" services. Besides that, the core services offered by ICT Service Provider organizations include telecommunications (TSPs); software application service (ASPs); internet service (ISPs); cloud services (CSPs); network services (NSPs); and storage services (SSPs).

"Service Providers" (SP) as a term is suggestive of a unit, group or organization whose major function is to provide a defined service. By this, it means that virtually every unit or sub-unit in an organization literally qualifies to bear that nomenclature. But in ICT and management consulting, "service provider" connotes a larger context which is more specific, specialized and unique. For instance, communication through telephones is a specialized, huge infrastructural investment business. Not everyone who has the competence or knowledge about the telecommunication system can provide the service. Also, no business except one fully invested in commercial telecom service provision can afford to wholly own its business telecommunication infrastructure to connect to the outer world. A business can at best have an internal PABX or VoIP (Voice over Internet Protocol) system which ends within the boundaries of the business premises. Such large conglomerates like AT&T, Verizon, Sprint, MTN, and Vodacom among so many others are telecommunication Service Providers positioned for such services. The same holds true for other service areas like internet connectivity service, servers and data centers; cloud computing, software as a service (SaaS) or application services.

Moreover, even where a service can be sourced in-house (Internal Service Providers), every business evaluates the comparative advantage in setting up, staffing, funding, operating and administering a particular service as against outsourcing it (to External Service Providers). As for Shared Services, IT services or resources which hitherto were the exclusive preserve of one part of an organization is shared with the whole or more parts of the organization, thereby distributing the burden of funding and resourcing of that service being shared. When this happens, the originating unit for that service or resource becomes known as an internal service provider.

By ITIL standards, the service provider categories are rated as Type I, Type II and Type III respectively for internal service providers, shared service providers and external service providers[2].

External service providers provide IT services to external customers. They use what is regarded as managed services or Managed Service Providers to provide full outsourced IT service to an organization or a limited range service such as delivering a product feature, a software application, network administration, data warehousing and so on.

IT Service Provider organizations have similar features as IT Original Equipment Manufacturers (OEMs) and Vendors. The difference between them is in the power of choice OEMs/Vendors have, to decide whether to provide accompanying support services such as "IT consulting" and other professional services with customer orders and supplies. Companies that provide accompanying support services belong to both categories while others that strictly sell their equipment/software without accompanying support services belong specifically to the latter category.

The size of IT Service Provider organizations are in the region of thousands of employees with global presence across several countries and regions worldwide. This type of ICT organizations shape IT industry standards and trends; funding organized research and development efforts either for their own products and services or those of OEMs and software manufacturers. Therefore, they attract and retain the best brains in the industry.

A career in a service provider organization is a privileged opportunity to play in the big league; learning from among the finest breed of professionals while also exposed to the finest details of technology. Besides working and learning – working under the tutelage of higher team members – one can be sure of access to standard world-class training opportunities conducted by industry technology experts and leaders in product development and research. This is different from what one might have access to in a strictly IT consulting outfit where exploiting employee skills to enhance business profitability may actually be the only primary goal – especially in smaller IT consulting firms.

IT service providers are akin to teaching hospitals in the medical field. In some cases, after retirement from a long running career in a service provider organization, some professionals subsequently setup IT consulting firms in their knowledge area of strength.

IT service providers deal mostly with large corporations, national and international government institutions, agencies or parastatals; multinationals, conglomerates; large religious, political and academic campuses and other big corporate organizations.

Organizations of this nature and magnitude are usually large ICT consumers. IT service providers usually decide what category of clientele to service based on certain formal or informal criteria namely;

- IT skills capacity – some recommend and follow up with verifications of employment in the organization, of professionals who have earned the license, training level and certification of the Service Provider's or that of a related industry equivalent (sometimes strictly the certification of that specific service provider).
- Project scope
- Number of employees or workstations and geographic spread of the organization
- Financial capacity – which is also 'self-determining' by the organization, especially if the service provider attaches certain subscription or maintenance based contract terms and conditions.
- Security, local or international government regulatory frameworks, socio-cultural and legal limitations built into service provision terms and conditions.

Finally, IT service providers focus on ICT infrastructure and operations; therefore they operate in the industry through a combination of these service systems;

- IT consulting services
- Managed Service Provider systems whereby they provide whole or part IT services to an organization
- Hardware or software IT resource or product supply or lease; subscription service; hosting; warehousing; storage/archiving; or maintenance contract

And some of the services they provide through these service systems include;

- ✓ Big data solutions and services
- ✓ Cloud computing/storage services
- ✓ Commercial generic or bespoke application software development
- ✓ Data center solutions
- ✓ Franchise IT procurement vendors
- ✓ Hosting services
- ✓ Internet Service provision
- ✓ IT payment processor solutions
- ✓ Manufacturing (IT hardware or software)
- ✓ Migration/integration services
- ✓ Outsourced IT services
- ✓ Network support solutions
- ✓ Telecommunication services

<u>11</u>

ICT OEMs and Vendor Organizations

The global information and communication technology system runs on the backbone of numerous hardware and software technologies manufactured or developed by original equipment manufacturers (OEMs). The ICT industry therefore is the engine room or the heart and brain behind the global information system.

The ICT industry dictates the trends, standards and overall pace of growth of the information and communication system. By implication, the ICT industry is behind the revolution in business systems; social, economic, cultural and political trends like lifestyles and entertainment; healthcare, agriculture and almost every other industrial sector on earth.

As I pointed out earlier, ICT as a "child-discipline" from the root foundational bodies of knowledge for ICT has given essence – life and significance – to those disciplines from which it sprouted. Just as consumer electronics industry once gave essence and significance to electrical engineering (for what is electricity or electrical energy good for, if its generation, presence or existence has no essential utility value to life?), so also ICT has done to its mother-root disciplines. Defining the ICT industry without the inclusion of its essential, inextricable root-disciplines' industrial base would render an incomplete ambiguous description because ICT OEMs/Vendor organizations are a big part of both worlds.

ICT OEMs/Vendors are inventors and innovators of products, associated infrastructure as well as new technologies. They discover knowledge concepts and principles and package them together into working-knowledge; create technology systems with its associated infrastructure and end-user products or services. At the core of these activities are systemized, global web of research and development programs teeming with thousands if not millions of scientists.

As much as OEMs/Vendor organizations produce the underlying technologies and products that define the information system, they are also consumers of IT for the purpose of running their organized business systems. Therefore they are among the "ICT Consumer Organizations" we shall be discussing next. Without their using the products and technologies they are building, how will they understand or have a feel of what the customer for whom they are inventing a product, service or solution experiences? How will they understand how to make it better?

ICT OEMs/Vendors concentrate on their core competencies in most cases while outsourcing a number of functions outside their core competences to "IT Service Providers". This way, they are less distracted by non-essential services. It is not always in their best interest for manufacturing companies to take on "Service Provider" functions alongside their production activities although a few may serve as both, sometimes using subsidiaries. "IT Vendors" are sometimes franchises, subsidiaries or what is known as "resellers" for major OEMs.

For instance, Microsoft - a large software manufacturing organization whose core competencies include; creating high-volume software products, working with other software companies, and providing customer service and support - outsource some of their organization's IT or other functions. Bill Gates said that, "*we outsource a number of functions*" that do not fall into those core competencies. The functions they outsource according to him are "*help-desk technical support for our employees*" and "*physical production of our software packages*"[3].

Working for an IT OEM organization is a rare privilege for any aspiring professional. It is akin to working in a service provider organization, different perhaps only in the degree to which specialization renders one's capacity to be versatile slim. But if you sought it, you should love it. Most OEM's "core" personnel are invested in the organization for the long haul and the organization massively invests in them, their talents and skills pretty well.

Let us wrap up this section by taking a quick random peek at six organizations as examples of some of the major ICT industry technology OEMs/Vendors; their employee size, products and services to drive home this section. Some of them include the following;

AT&T Inc. is an American multinational telecommunications conglomerate with several subsidiaries including AT&T Digital life, Cricket Wireless, Otter Media; AT&T Mobility and AT&T U-Verse. AT&T products include mobile phones, fixed-line phones, satellite and digital television, internet broadband and home security. Through subsidiaries like U-Verse and Cricket Wireless, AT&T produces mobile phones, tablets, mobile broadband devices and wireless communication; through AT&T Digital Life, home security and home automation devices are manufactured while Otter Media provides OTT services, online TV programming and Digital Networks. AT&T has 273 thousand employees worldwide[4]. Other Giants in similar line of products and services are Verizon, Sprint, Orange, T-Mobile, O_2, Vodafone, Vodacom and other global and national telecoms products manufacturers and service providers.

Apple Inc. is quoted as the largest Information and Communication Technology Company in the world by revenue; the world's largest technology company by assets; and the world's second-largest mobile phone manufacturer by volume after Samsung[5]. Apple's line of products covers computers, mobile (smart) phones and tablets, pads, and operating systems with the iOS and Macintosh (Mac) brands; services including cloud computing through iCloud. They also have internet software application services that offer online marketing services like iTunes and the Apple store. Like most OEMs, they also have subsidiaries one of which is Beats Electronics they acquired in 2015; and an employee size of 116,000 as at October 2016[6]. Other brands in the same line of products are Samsung, Google (Nexus), Nokia, HTC, Sony and so on.

Cisco is an industry leader in network infrastructure equipment. Cisco develops, manufactures, and sells networking hardware, telecommunications equipment, and other high-technology services and products like switches, gateways, routers, security firewall hardware and software; intrusion prevention and intrusion defense systems (IPS/IDS); wireless network devices, IP phones and so on. Cisco is the world's leader in enterprise networking with a massive install base across multiple platform product categories worldwide.

Like most OEMs, Cisco also owns subsidiaries and is a big player in specialized technology markets in the area of "Internet of Things" (IoT), energy management and domain security. Cisco has also delved into the cloud and software market with the introduction this February, 2017 of a product known as Cisco Umbrella, a cloud-based internet gateway for safeguarding against cloud and mobile security risks especially when bypassing VPN or corporate network connections to connect to Data centers[7].

Employee size is quoted as 71, 883 as at 2016[8]. In competition in their line of business are companies like HP, Huawei, Juniper Networks, Avaya and Alcatel-Lucent (currently absorbed into Nokia Networks as a recent acquisition).

Google is another American multinational technology company involved in manufacturing hardware and software platforms, products and services. It started out as just Google, but now a leading subsidiary of Alphabet Corporation focused on Alphabet's Internet business interests. Google is popular for its Google Search technology but boasts of several other internet application services such as cloud computing, online advertising technologies; business services such as Google Docs, Sheets and Slides; email application services, Google Calendar, Google Drive, Google+; instant messaging and video chat apps like Hangout, Duo; language translation through Google Translate and Google Maps for navigation and mapping. Others are Blogger, Google Keep and Google Photos.

Google also ventured into hardware products manufacturing with the development of the Android mobile operating system. This they achieved through partnerships with major electronics OEMs leading to the introduction of Nexus smartphone devices,

Home smart speakers, Wi-Fi mesh wireless routers and Daydream view virtual reality headsets[9].

Google also produced the Chrome web browser, and Chrome Operating System, a lightweight operating system based on the Chrome browser.

The products and services are numerous and hopefully will continue to grow as technology advances for a conglomerate with a mission statement that says they want *"to organize the world's information and make it universally accessible and useful"*[10].

Google's employee size as at quarter two, 2015 stood at 57, 100[11].

IBM (International Business Machines) Corporation is also an American multinational technology company with operations in over 170 countries and one of the world's largest employers with about 380, 000 employees[12].

IBM's manufactured product line and patents are too numerous to list here. It is said of the company that it has the largest number of patents by any single business[13]. Some of IBM's hardware and software inventions, products and services include computers, middleware and software; the invention of the automated teller machine (ATM), Personal Computer, SQL programming language, Hard/Floppy Disk Drives, DRAM, and the relational database among others. IBM also provides hosting and consulting services in nanotechnology and mainframe computers.

IBM is not left out in the industry's acquisitions of subsidiary companies and through theirs, offers services such as cloud computing, cognitive computing, IoT (Internet of Things), big data and analytics; others are in IT infrastructure, mobile, security, IBM SaaS (Software as a Service), IaaS (Infrastructure as a Service) and PaaS (Platform as a Service) all offered through cloud delivery models (public, hybrid and private). As I said earlier, the hardware products are too numerous to list here, ranging from microprocessor chips to encryption hardware products.

IBM owns more than 40 data centers globally and is leading in technology research for the future. The company is investing billions of dollars into building a chip than can imitate the workings of the human brain - how about that! So if you are researching the kinds of tech companies you would love to join their team to do exciting things, this is one[14].

Citrix Systems Inc. is an American multinational software company that services around 330,000 organizations worldwide. That is a huge business portfolio! As an OEM, service providers act as vendors using the Citrix products line to meet customer demands.

Citrix has an employee base of about 9,500 and produces server, application and desktop virtualization, networking, and cloud computing technologies.

Citrix's software products are designed to enable enterprise workers to remotely function and collaborate irrespective of the device or network they use. Their major focus is on desktops and apps; providing services such as Desktop as a Service (DaaS); networking and cloud service; and Software as a Service (SaaS).

Some of their software tools include Citrix XenApp, Citrix XenDesktop, and Citrix VDI-in-a-Box which provides application virtualization allowing users to gain access remotely to their desktops and networks. Cloud based Citrix Workspace provides the platform for building and delivering desktops and application from the cloud. There is XenMobile, WorxMobile, AppDNA, Citrix Receiver, and their file sharing app, ShareFile. For networking and the cloud, we also have Citrix XenServer, NetScaler and Application Delivery Controllers (ADC); Gateways, AppFirewall and others[15].

These few sample OEMs/Vendor companies mentioned is just to provide an insight into the nature and organization of their businesses as earlier explained. I could go on and on because there is several thousand of this type of organization worldwide; some important names like Intel, Broadcom, Microsoft, Checkpoint, Dell, and A10 among many others all fit into this category of ICT organizations.

12

ICT Consumer Organizations

Customers and end users of the ICT resource on a personal or particularly business scale are ICT consumer organizations and that includes all the preceding classes of ICT organizations discussed.

ICT Consumption cuts across every stratum of personal life and business and that is the purpose of information and communication technology; to serve as a tool for living and business.

ICT consumer organizations are in various sizes ranging from small, medium to large-scale organizations. A small scale firm can range from one self employed registered business owner to 10-50 employees with one or multiple IT products and services being utilized to enable the business perform its functions to customers.

The increasing use of innovative IT software and hardware solutions to power business operations provides enormous opportunities for IT knowledge workers worldwide; hence, the corresponding increase in demand for IT skills globally. Every business today, at one level or the other directly or indirectly employs one or more IT professionals for one or more professional services. Indirectly for instance, the existence of phone call services guarantees that IT professionals are employed by telecom service providers. A business that is not fully invested in ICT systems would still intermittently - as the need arises - require the services of an IT firm or freelance IT professionals.

Therefore whether the organization is a business focused on healthcare services, agriculture, cosmetics, food and beverages; or a departmental store, a clothing store, or any other kind of business; either a multinational or a single branch office business, provided in one way or more it leverages the tools of information and communication technology to power a part or whole of its business operations, it is an ICT consumer organization.

Having had an overview of what kinds of organizations provide the latitude and platforms for practicing IT, it is good to observe how the organizations shift their focus from time to time in line with technology advancements and trends; from one product or service offering to another. Also worthy of note are the various prevailing products and services in the industry ranging from communications, internet technologies, networking, software applications, computer hardware and software, microchips technologies, servers and gateways, security devices and software, database, cloud computing, IT infrastructure, virtual technologies, mobility, computer games and social media to various kinds and levels of service provision and consultancies.

13

ICT Skills Marketplaces

The skills marketplace for IT professionals is not much different from the overall job market which comprises of the demand and supply of skills for all industry sectors except that there is a higher demand for IT professionals in almost all industry sector and a seeming shortage of specialty IT skilled professionals in certain knowledge areas.

The buyers are any one of the categories of ICT organizations while the sellers are the ICT skilled professionals; either as paid employees or as freelance professionals.

To succeed or survive in this marketplace, one must possess real IT skills and be consciously aware of his or her IT skill level; what it is worth and for which kind of ICT organization it would be suitable, both for the buyer and the seller. This is important because it engenders confidence which is critical to win the trust of an intending buyer (employer). It is what separates those with "bare certificates" from those who have both "certificates and skills".

There is a world of difference between having a broad spectrum of knowledge – general knowledge of the ICT profession's bodies of knowledge – and having usable IT skills in specific or specialized knowledge areas. For instance, one might have studied and earned certificates or certifications in information technology; possibly a master's degree but a potential employer would only be interested in one's ability to create and administer a website or web applications, infusing classic graphics designs into them for a number of clients with varying tastes. A professional must therefore above all else acquire easily practicable skills which meets specific cross-cutting needs of potential employers in the skills market.

Analyzing the histories and operations of most of the big industry players in ICT, one would realize that these companies consistently innovate with changing technology trends. Those that fail to move at the same pace with prevailing technology trends are bound to be out of business overtime. At the moment, cloud computing technologies and big data are gaining momentum and most, if not all OEMs are changing their business focus towards the trend. This is a lesson for all professionals also to be consistent in updating with new knowledge and skills as the needs of the market dictates in order to remain relevant. It may not be possible in all areas but at least, in line with one's IT career interests and goals.

Understand that there can be no such thing as "General IT practice", especially at entry and mid-career levels. Essentially at such levels, one is expected to understand the various ICT concepts as a broad discipline. But even Strasser in 1985 said,

"ICT is a practical science"[16] and that is how it is in reality. There cannot be action without an underlying knowledge base; facts, theories and principles; but the accurate application of these knowledge bodies in a specific area or ICT domain is the most essential expression of skill. That is why every entrant into the ICT field must acquire much breadth of its broad knowledge base before pursuing a specialization area.

Broader and deeper scope IT knowledge is also essential and most appreciated at top IT senior management levels for professionals who have seen it all, done it all (not necessarily "all", but have covered enough breadth) and therefore lead by virtue of experience and a web of skill sets.

The IT skills market is very competitive. To gain entry and grow, one must be ready to transform theoretical knowledge into practice that creates solutions. The market outlook at this time of writing highly favors professionals with a combination of competent knowledge, skills, experience and lastly certifications in cloud computing technologies, virtualization, software engineering; cyber, information and network security; networking (especially wireless networking); and a combination of ITIL and PMP certifications for administration and management level positions. What is required are experience, hands-on practice and real industry exposure coupled with the relevant certifications which validates the knowledge and skills possessed and also prove one's dedication to the IT trade. There is also demand for big data certifications and specialists in social media apps development with java programming skills.

It is important to note that there are one or more IT skills that will remain relevant for all times. These kinds of skills never go out of fashion and present veritable opportunities for entry level professionals lacking in experience and industry exposure for core function practice. Every ICT compliant organization has either intermittent or continuous need for such competencies in-house or outsourced to service providers. Most new entrants to IT field waste a number of years seeking the big league companies (there's no harm in trying, anyway). I would recommend <u>researching</u> and finding the small IT firms servicing the needs of large corporations even if it is for "peanuts" salary or as an intern. Evidently, from earlier sections on "ICT organizations", an organization has core-function ICT skill areas required for fulfilling IT/business goals and also ICT operations services and service management skills area required for the smooth operation and survival of the information/business system. IT help desk, hardware and software installations, configurations, maintenance, networking and other related services belong in this group.

For instance, financial institutions require core IT staff at their headquarters who have core IT skills like in database management systems, enterprise server knowledge, enterprise network experts, enterprise security experts; or staff with knowledge, skills and certifications of specific OEM's ERM (Enterprise Resource Management), ERP (Enterprise Resource Planning) or other specialist software (e.g. Microsoft, Oracle, SAP, Checkpoint, or vendor-neutral Linux and so on); and also end user basic computing skills (which in most cases are entry level requirements for other knowledge workers at the desktop level). But the overall system maintenance; software upgrades and patches, device installations and configurations, network extensions, fault escalation, diagnostics and repairs (where it is an accepted policy because most large organizations replace instead of repair); and all other services that keep the IT system running smoothly are reserved for a specific department or in some cases outsourced to external service providers. In some organizations like in the oil and gas industries, key IT projects and services are usually outsourced even as they maintain fully staffed IT departments. The IT departments mainly act as interface between the organization and external service providers; streamlining organizational IT policy frameworks with their operations while safeguarding business' IT assets against vulnerabilities.

Therefore at entry level, homing in the right IT skills that match your knowledge based profile and well determined IT career trajectory would help you exude that confidence needed to win that interview and land the job. Any degree or certification is worthless without adequate skills and competence to justify it. Academic degrees and vendor-specific certifications may help you get to the door, but it wouldn't get you past that door or if it does, sustain you through your career if your only objective during the IT education process was just about earning a certification by memorizing "exam dumps", or cramming without the accompanying practical skills. Learn the technology, internalize it and if possible find free voluntary job opportunities or internships that provide practical platforms to learn. In the final chapter of this book, we shall enumerate some practical steps and ideas a "newbie" can take which can help sharpen his or her skills and even result in earned income.

Finally, a professional who combines specialization in a specific ICT domain with relevant breadth of ICT knowledge has more employment opportunities, and occupies a competitive position on the market. This is because although "ICT depth" has been of utmost focus in recent times, it is also necessary to create the right balance between both, by having adequate "ICT breadth" of knowledge. In reality, although ICT professionals have very much in common, yet they have different job profiles. When one understands deeply the categories of ICT organizations, their modes of operation and activities coupled with knowledge of ICT foundational bodies of knowledge and knowledge building blocks; through careful logical analysis, it is easy to understand the market dynamics relative to the skills one possesses or should pursue. When that is done properly, successfully finding a job or engaging in private practice in the industry would be as easy as eating a piece of cake. The question then remains; do you have what it takes? Have you gotten what it takes? And, are you pursuing or ready to pursue what it takes?

14

ICT Skill-Levels

Whereas "knowledge" - ICT knowledge - refers to underlying bodies of established facts, theories, principles and methodologies; an ICT skill draws or extracts from that "knowledge" for a practical ICT problem-solving application. Knowledge carries within it potentials or possibilities while skill(s) is knowledge in action and has various levels of application.

In the military and other regimental institutions, there are usually rankings for personnel according to their levels of training, responsibilities, year of enlistment into service, and influence; sometimes also dependent on an exceptionally accomplished mission or task, from the bottom to the top. So, ranking is not new and is an acknowledgement of the importance of growth or progression in a career path.

Similarly in ICT, although not so much a strictly formal process like in the regimental system, every IT professional is recognized and rated according to skill levels, but particularly relative to a specialty knowledge area. What this means for instance is that a level 5 security certified professional may also be a level 2 network or database management professional and vice versa. It is therefore dependent on what level of mastery a professional develops and deploys which must be validated by a duly recognized certifying authority evidenced by a certificate.

This certifying authority may either be a national, regional or international regulatory body; a professional association or a product OEM/Vendor's certification program.

Certification programs also follow a bottom-top approach; what they call certification tracks. The tracks represent levels of skill achievement, sometimes with prerequisites in between for achieving higher certifications on the ladder. The ratings are usually an expression of the differences in levels of responsibility, accountability and effectiveness in exercising a skill.

For example, Australia developed what is known as the Skills Framework for the Information Age (SFIA). This SFIA has been adopted in about 200 countries in the world as it best represents the global nature of ICT profession[17]. The SFIA provides a tabular construct with a two dimensional matrix. One axis consists of SFIA skills grouped by categories and subcategories. The second axis consists of the different levels of responsibility and accountability at which ICT practitioners can exercise each skill. The second axis is defined using the seven levels listed in Table 3.1. According to the SFIA skills classification, a skill is rated to be practiced under close supervision at level 1 while level 7 skills are practiced in a leadership capacity in which the ICT professional leads, manages or influences others. Other parameters apart from autonomy and influence used to gauge a skill level are complexity and business skills[18].

SFIA Level	Description of level of autonomy and responsibility
1	Follow
2	Assist
3	Apply
4	Enable
5	Ensure, advise
6	Initiate, influence
7	Set strategy, inspire, mobilize

Table 3: SFIA Levels of Autonomy and Responsibility Axis (SFIA, 2011)

However, it is not expected that an ICT professional who just graduated from an academic program in a higher institution would begin at the bottom. Graduates are expected to begin at level 4, in some cases at level 5.

Skill levels may also be rated as beginner, intermediate, professional and expert; or as associate, professional, expert, master or architect levels. Whichever nomenclature is adopted, it is an indication of a progression towards maturity.

One other important characteristic of IT skill levels is that it is dynamic. A professional must keep abreast with updated knowledge and skills to remain relevant in the industry.

"An investment in knowledge always pays the best interest"

~ Benjamin Franklin

Four

ICT Education and Training

15

All Your Learning Options

ICT Education and training comprises of the various formal and informal modes of learning and practical skills acquisition. The most fundamental ICT education begins when one achieves a certification through undergoing a formal course of study in any of the *"root foundational bodies of knowledge for ICT"* or the *"ICT foundational bodies of knowledge"* disciplines in any academic institution of higher learning.

The base knowledge or core specializations are usually gained from the formal or traditional academic institutions of higher learning while ICT "continuing education" programs are usually sourced mainly from the private sector where organizations or individuals set up, manage and organize a talent pool of IT professionals as resource persons for the purpose of ICT training and education. Some OEMs/Vendors also run their own fully organized and managed "University" or academies; some grant licensed academic and practical laboratory course materials, curriculum and credentials to private investors who meet their accreditation. However, one of the most cost effective, often embraced programs for ICT "continuing education", especially by "already active" IT professionals is self-study.

ICT continuing education programs addresses specific industry's skills requirements "on the go" as new technologies emerge; also when complex products with extensive knowledge features, configurations, systematic installations and maintenance routines are introduced which requires the continuous support of specially trained personnel. Some programs also focus on either an ICT industry regulation protocol or any of "ICT management" protocols in specific areas with vast knowledge base which are usually not covered in details in the academic institutions.

Finally, some programs are industry professional association programs which culminate in an examination, for which a certificate of recognition into standard membership for practice is given to successful candidates. Whichever one or more of these continuing education programs anyone decides to pursue, he or she must ensure that it is aligned with his or her career objectives.

Some examples of OEM's universities are Oracle University, Cisco University (also part of Cisco Academies worldwide), Microsoft Virtual Academy, and Microsoft Office 365 University and so on.

In the sections below, we shall examine the informal learning options for ICT continuing education so that one may be able to evaluate his or her circumstances in making a decision about which option(s) is most helpful.

The more formal or traditional "brick and mortar" education through academic institutions is obviously the first option for ICT education and what it entails has already been covered, if you have been following this book sequentially, in both sections; the *"root foundational bodies of knowledge for ICT"* and *"ICT foundational bodies of knowledge"*. If it was not particularly clear at that stage, you may revert back to those sections to understand better; and while reviewing, understand that the *root foundational bodies of knowledge for ICT* and a great majority of the *ICT foundational bodies of knowledge* are usually learned from academic institutions of higher learning at bachelor's, master's or PHD degree levels depending on the strength of the institution's program design.

The Informal Sector Learning Options

Firstly, let's not mistake the word "informal" for something less serious or off the record. By "informal", is to indicate that the methods used for acquiring ICT education are different from the traditional system which rates and recognizes an individual as someone who has acquired a standardized formal education. And that is why, regardless of whatever other certification or skill anyone may have, the minimum qualification for most IT jobs in any corporate organization starts with the bachelor's degree.

ICT Firms

The informal ICT continuing education sector consists of many players, some of which are ICT service management organizations or ICT consulting firms with an educational arm. They usually offer a multifaceted stream of diverse IT vendors' certification programs; sometimes either in liaison with credential owners to deliver their course contents as authorized training centers or independently by just using their talent pool of certified professionals to deliver the courses, combining that with their provision of IT consulting services to clients. The advantages of this kind of setup to the student are;

i.   The trainees have the benefit of learning from field experienced professionals who are actively using the technology they are teaching about, rather than teaching what they have only read from text books.

ii.   The trainees may enjoy internship opportunities through the trainers by being part of some of the firm's IT projects.

iii. Exceptionally performing trainees might be lucky to be retained as employees.

Franchise Training Providers

This category is just like the ICT firms discussed above only that they are specifically small or large-scale registered or licensed training providers focused only on IT education. They usually have a network of hundreds or thousands of branches globally and maybe usually focused on just one or fewer vendors' certification tracks.

Franchise training providers sometimes also act as exam testing centers for the vendor; in some cases a candidate might get discounts on exam fees. Some others may be a registered Pearson VUE, Prometric or other testing service center, giving the student the benefit of becoming accustomed to and comfortable with the testing environment before the exam day.

Small Business Training Institutes

There are many - especially in most developing countries – training outfits that are very small businesses engaged in one or a few aspects of ICT services or product sales that provide commercial unlicensed, unregistered training to interested candidates, provided the candidate trusts the proficiency level of their trainers; after which they may go ahead to sit for the appropriate relevant certification exams. These training centers are no different from the big ICT firms in their training services. The difference lies in the corporate outlook, business scale, available training equipment and perceived integrity and quality of service. Be aware that in highly organized societies, running unlicensed or unregistered training services may be in breach of statutory regulations.

While the training resources available and the corporate integrity of an outfit are very significant factors in choosing a training outfit, sometimes reputation as a prime factor may overshadow quality in such a way that what one gets pales in comparison with the huge training fees paid. Some get to be over-subscribed with lesser student to trainer rapport.

In a smaller instructor-led training (ILT) setup, trainees usually have closer communication and interaction both with their instructor and among themselves which enhances understanding. Where subscription numbers are not controlled as a policy, lower training costs may have the effect of driving trainee enrollment up. Hence, the overriding decision factor for a trainee should be to find a good training setup with smaller classes whether in a big or small firm. In addition to that is the level of expertise and experience of the trainers combined with available training materials given to the trainee during training. The available equipment for the practice sessions should also rank high in one's considerations.

I must point out that your IT training needs can be met by just about any IT professional or expert on an individual basis, in an informal setting. It doesn't have to be in an organized setup; it can be by a person-to-person arrangement, fee based or for free depending on the willingness and availability of the professional or expert. What matters is that at the end of the day, you end up learning something tangible and helpful.

Virtual Learning Web Portals

Virtual web-based learning (e-learning) provides for anytime, anywhere education. This mode of learning is already being adopted by some traditional, established universities worldwide as their online university arm for expanded access to education. The beauty of it is that entry requirements for undergraduate programs are either non-restrictive or totally absent. It is a very flexible system and affords candidates the opportunity to work, learn and earn certificates.

However for IT continuing education programs, virtual web-based learning is a veritable source for home based, independent self-study type of learning. Trainings on a variety of subject matters are focused on practical ICT technology routines (installation procedures, configuration routines, technical concepts, administration, architecture and so on) especially with regards to diverse IT vendors' products (software and hardware). General theoretical knowledge is also covered within textual information, made available through printed or eBook course materials which the trainees can study independently at their own schedule.

Training videos are usually made available on these portals which the student can download or stream online. It is better when a video is downloaded for continuous study reviews time and again. There are also opportunities to link up with the trainers for question and answer sessions through chats; discussion forums with other students and sharing of exams or work related success tips and resources are also available.

Independent Self Study

As the title suggests, personal responsibility to studies; study materials, pace, practical sessions, examination date and time for achieving certification are all at the behest of the individual.

Self-study methods of learning, like others culminates in standard examinations conducted through computer based tests (CBT). CBTs are usually managed by accredited globally recognized testing providers on behalf of credential owners.

Therefore, any testing service that proctors any exam is usually a pre-determined choice made by the owners of the exam credentials one is seeking.

Self study connotes the ability of an interested candidate for a professional certification course and exam to seek out and learn through relevant course materials; practice labs, practice exam questions; audio and video CD-ROMs, printed books or eBooks and business-case example studies; or any other material that can aid in learning the theory, concepts and technology of interest and passing its exams, on his or her own.

Self study requires a lot of discipline and self motivation for success. There must be first and foremost a huge desire for the very expertise or skill being sought after to make a success out of it, more than passing the exams. One must relish in the honor, recognition and opportunities inherent in becoming a member of an elite group of IT professionals possessing the relevant certification required at each cadre (skill level) of a vendor-specific or vendor-neutral, industry recognized IT credential. That is enough fuel to fire up one's motivation.

Note that at the certification entry-level across all vendor platforms for any core IT specialty area, general knowledge about the concepts, theories and principles of that specialization which each vendor product (software or hardware) addresses are usually covered. This is why each vendor's first (entry-level) certification track usually serves as prerequisites for other higher level certifications on the ladder.

One challenge an entrant into IT certifications and learning may face at the initial stage is the availability and access to free self study resources. Some course materials are readily available for free download from the internet. A simple Google search will produce several results, some of which can be useful. Some vendors or credential owners closely guard access to their study materials and only make them available to their authorized training centers (ATCs). The ATCs might as well protect the resources from circulation. How successful this can be in a world where sharing digital resources are only a click away is another story altogether.

But as soon as that hurdle is scaled, the next challenge is in the ability of the student to be very imaginative. Self study is much easier for people whose imaginative faculties and capacity are fully developed. This is because IT vendor certifications are focused on real life scenarios concerning real technology products as tools for solving business problems. They deal practically with the installation, configuration, usage or administration, troubleshooting and maintenance of these IT tools in enterprise environments. The student must therefore study with an "imaginary" application mindset and where possible find ways to simulate the business case scenarios. This is why some, if not all vendors recommend between 6-12 months work within the industry where the software or hardware is in use before sitting for certain tracks of their certifications especially after the entry level track.

But we also know that in reality, an aspiring professional may just be trying to launch an entry into IT career in a specialty area; might be working in IT already but aspiring for other IT specialist roles; or someone who might have lost a job, therefore attempting a new knowledge and skill for "in-demand" IT job roles. Therefore gaining access to the hardware, software or work environment necessary for real hands-on practice may not be feasible. Faced with such situations, one option is to enroll into any of the vendors' authorized training centers or other informal IT learning institutes across the various cities of the world.

Along with this option comes the challenge of costs. IT continuing education does come with a price tag, even for taking the CBT exams. Again, even where a candidate can afford a local training center, there still are some certifications whereby out of the vendor's list of authorized training centers worldwide, an interested candidate's country may not have ATC availability – that is, none available in that country or region. For instance Check Point, an industry leader in IT Security does not currently have any authorized training center in Nigeria; even in the whole of Africa, only South Africa has authorized training centers. This, kind of places more financial burden on intending candidates to attend 4-5 days training by travelling to South Africa for the course. In some other cases, like the Cisco Certified Internetwork Expert (CCIE) and other advanced level certifications which require a vendor's closer monitoring of the exams as well as special business case lab-equipped testing environments, designated exam countries are usually specified which also adds to the costs of acquiring the certification.

All these nonetheless are challenges which any serious candidate or professional can overcome. Whether you are in a financial position to afford it or not is of no significance if you set your heart to it. It is easier if one has a job, a good savings or other financial sponsorship. But one must not forget that someone who has a job also has not much time and focus which is very crucial for studies. If you do have both time and some sort of financial sponsorship, then you've got something very precious. Some big IT companies do sponsor their IT staff especially when acquiring a vendor's IT platform solutions as part of the sales agreements or pre-conditions. But the motivational strength that comes with having none at all, yet with a willingness to find the means even if it's the last cash you've got moves mountains for you. I guess I am speaking to students or out-of-job graduates here. Be and stay motivated towards your well defined purpose, starting with the least resource you can get. Search on the internet, find support forums, make friends on the same track and you will find people perhaps ahead of you who would assist you and send study materials or other resources your way for free. When you are truly ready for your life's purpose, the heavens would open up for you. But first, THIRST!

Self study is very interesting. Personally I love and enjoy it – teaching myself new technology is usually fun for me. But there's a place for interactive learning which is where community learning comes in. There are some persons who draw energy from interacting with people of similar pursuits. People who are good with self study are usually sapped of energy in learning environments with large human interactivity – it is an energy draining exercise for them. They are mainly introverted in nature, at their best when alone, locked in their own world and thoughts. It therefore is important that you understand what works best for you; a good training center may not always be feasible due to costs, convenience or availability, which leaves someone with the choice of independent self study. In such situations, it is advisable to seek out audio-visual materials or subscribe for web-based virtual learning.

Let me recommend a few top web-based IT virtual learning portals with access to audio and visual learning resources. Most of them have great archives of audio and video recordings on various certifications' technology with practical demonstrations. These leading IT resource websites include the following;

- *CBT Nuggets*: One of the leading online IT training portals focused on key IT vendors' technologies and provides practice test exams, virtual labs for hands-on practice, access to training videos and even the opportunity to have a personal coach. The quality of their training methods and instructors are top notch.
- *Udemy* is a global online learning marketplace where students master new skills; learning from an extensive library of about 45,000 courses covering a wide variety of subjects and courses. IT certification courses from various vendors are covered in their training services with costs ranging from $10-$500.
- *Simplilearn* is another online IT training portal worthy of mention. Simplilearn.com offers strictly IT core courses and certifications.

For more information visit http://www.simplilearn.com
- *Lynda* is also a subscription-based online IT training website with a large video tutorial library. If you are more visual oriented, this site is a good resource base for your needs. With $25 monthly subscription, one could gain access to over 80,000 videos on a broad range of subjects and courses.

For more information, visit http://www.lynda.com.

- *Codecademy* is another online learning resource website focused strictly on software coding using various programming languages.

For more information, visit their website at http://www.codecademy.com.

- *Udacity* offers limited but quality in-demand skills such as in Data Sciences, Artificial Intelligence, Machine learning, Android, iOS and more. It has a strong technology focus. Other areas are robotics, software programming, digital marketing and web development courses.

For more information and reviews, visit their website at http://www.udacity.com.

You may also check out Bloc and Skillshare. Finally, YouTube is a great place to find resources if you know the specific course or technology titles you wish to learn about.

Most IT training companies offer either instructor-led training (ILT) or computer-based test (CBT) mode of training or both. Always seek out those with suitable programs that satisfy your certification training requirements; and which best supports you in developing deeper insights in your choice knowledge area.

16

What is ICT (IT) Certification?

The word or phrase "Certification or IT Certification" have been mentioned severally in this book and it is my hope that at the very least, a reader understands that it refers primarily to an acquired credential or certificate of completion for any IT-related specialty knowledge and skill.

The definition above is clear enough. But certifications are not only characteristic to ICT; other professional industries also have their own credential programs for continuing education. It is also important to note that "certifications" are additional

<u>qualifications</u> for attaining and fulfilling industry job roles and responsibilities necessary for specific industry requirements for new knowledge, new skills and new validation credentials with ***ongoing*** technological advancements in the industry. They rarely serve corporate demands without primary entry qualifications backing them. However, certifications are veritable proofs of someone's current knowledge and skills' status; the person's preparedness and readiness to tackle head-on the challenges of any work environment.

Certifications, unlike academic institutions' degrees which are lifetime achievements are tenure-based and usually have validity periods ranging between 2-5 years at the discretion of the credential owners. It therefore means that acquiring an industry technology certification (vendor-specific or vendor-neutral) is not an end in itself; rather, it requires continuous maintenance of its validity through either re-certification or acquiring other higher but related certifications.

Indisputably, certifications are distinguishing elements in any professional's resume. It gives a professional an edge over other potential candidates for a job; be it as an employee or a consultant. It tells a potential employer that the candidate is a knowledge enthusiast who is committed to learning and professionalism. It also demonstrates initiative and remarkable capacity for growth. However, its potency in closing the deal is higher only if the certification in view for a particular job role matches the organization's skill requirement at the time, otherwise it may just be an unnecessary appendage.

The weight of an ICT credential is also determined by the current cutting-edge technology trend and how up-to-date a particular specialty IT credential or certification is at the time.

Therefore, it is important for any intending entrant to research the industry trend at the period relative to the specialization of interest and undertake a certification program according to relevance.

What differentiates a rigorous IT discipline's academic body of knowledge degree with IT certifications that someone is still required to possess a vendor certification in order to be considered for certain job roles? Not much I would say. Every vendor's technological product builds on the concepts, principles and theories of information technology. This is why two competing companies' products would be seeking to solve the same business problem in an enterprise. Each can serve for a specific application. However, as in life, no two individuals are the same or would do things the same way. So also are these products in the methods and techniques of their installations, configurations and administration. For instance, a company may deploy either a Cisco router and switch for their networks or a HP, Mikrotic, Juniper Networks or other vendor's products. For software, the company may go for Microsoft, Oracle, Informatica or SAP solutions and so on depending on which IT skill specialty of commonality is of interest. A specific configuration command-syntax can execute a similar or particular instruction in any given situation although created by different companies' teams of engineers using the same guiding engineering and programming language principles; yet that command-syntax is usually coded differently by different product brands.

Therefore, although a graduate ICT professional may understand the underlying technology behind the information system, specific ability required for gaining physical operational access into these ICT hardware and software assets; to integrate them effectively, managing and optimizing their features for operational effectiveness and efficiency is very essential. And that, my friend is what certification is all about!

17

Certifications' Skills Categories

According to Global Knowledge's research from a 2017 survey distributed globally on salary levels and market conditions for IT certifications which they summarized in a recent article on their website;

- *Security-related certifications pay on average over $17,000 per year more than the median IT certification salary.*
- *Citrix certifications have annual salaries that range from $99,411 to $105,086 with a median salary of $102,365.*
- *AWS Certified Solutions Architect – Associate is paying a median salary of $125,091.*
- *Project Management Professional (PMP) certifications are the most pervasive, with 730,000 active PMPs in 210 countries and territories worldwide.* [1]

Based on the foregoing information, it is obvious that IT qualifications boosted with certain relevant industry certifications are a ticket to vertical pay checks and career in IT. But more importantly, entrants or professionals need to first evaluate their primary motivating factor for seeking a particular career path before matching it with the earning potential inherent in it. This is because a job without passion would sooner lead to frustrations and under-performance on the job. Also, it is not enough to just earn the certificate; passion is a core ingredient for effectiveness and capacity building in any ICT skill category

Below are the various ICT skills categories that could serve to define for you, what area of expertise in actual ICT practice your chosen certification tracks and skills can be found as a choice career path. When you don't understand where you stand in the field; where your competencies are relevant, it is difficult to streamline your job search focus to organizations and job roles that will make the right fit for you and which will recognize the value and potentials in the skills you possess. Knowing what you have, where you are headed and what value proposition you intend to bring is essential in building that self confidence and insightful knowledge one needs to be a top choice candidate in an interview.

IT Infrastructure This skills category comprises of areas of expertise that are involved in the operation and control of an organization's IT infrastructure. An organization's IT infrastructure consists of the various hardware, software, all forms of stored data, and any wide area network (WAN) or local area network (LAN) equipment or both required for delivering and supporting her IT services and products.

The responsibilities of holders or intending holders of associated relevant credentials in this area of expertise includes technical preparation for business change management operations; managing the change process while maintaining regulatory, legal and professional standards; and creation and management of IT systems. Others are management of system components in virtual computing environments, performance monitoring and evaluation of systems and services relative to their impact on business, system or network security and sustainability.

IT Infrastructure specialty technologies and some relevant current certification paths for a career in this skill category include certifications concerned with the following;

- *Cloud Infrastructure*
- *Network Engineering and Administration*
- *Software Infrastructure*
- *System Administration and System Engineering*

Job roles include Project Lead, Network Engineer, System Engineer, IT Consultant and other equivalent titles.

Information management

Information management involves a comprehensive governance of decision support, business processes and digital services using all forms of structured and unstructured; internally and externally generated information. It covers strategy and policy making; the design of information structures and classifications, while setting policies for data sourcing and maintenance of the data content. It also involves the development of guidelines, procedures, working practices and training to promote compliance with regulatory frameworks for all aspects of data warehousing, data use and disclosure. Information management specialty technologies and some relevant certification paths for career in this skill category include tracks concerned with the following;

- *Database Administration and Development*
- *IT Documentation*
- *IT Project Management*
- *Scripting*
- *Server Administration*
- *Office Productivity*

Data management

Data management comprises of practices, procedures or processes that ensure the security, integrity, safety and availability of all forms of enterprise data and data structures that make up the organization's information systems. It involves all tools and skill-sets deployed for the management of data and information in all its forms; the analysis of information structures (including logical analysis of taxonomies, data and metadata); and the development of innovative ways of managing the information assets of the organization. Certification paths are similar to those of information management category.

Network Support

One's career path can be domiciled in the network support IT domain where skills and knowledge for the provision of network maintenance and support services are developed and deployed. Support may be provided to both end-users and the IT infrastructure system for its sustainability.

Network Support personnel typically investigate and resolve problems. They also monitor, report system performance and provide advice or training to users. They carry out fault corrections; optimize network performance and other necessary network designs, extensions and modifications to ensure an efficiently converged infrastructure from time to time.

Programming/ Software Development

One can be a developer as we shall see in several developer and architect certifications in the next section. It involves designing, building, testing and documentation of both new and modified software components from supplier specifications in accordance with agreed development and security standards and processes.

Systems Software

This category belongs to professionals with specialist software application skills, such as skills for any vendor-specific or vendor-neutral business application software or operating systems used in various organizations. They install, configure, maintain and administer various system software such as operating systems, data management products, personnel / resource / customer / supplier management software, office automation products and other utility software used across all ICT organizations.

Governance

Within this skill category are those skills that serve to streamline and integrate an organization's business requirements and strategy with its technology infrastructure, with the result that technology is effectively used to enforce policies, maintain oversight on business operations and direct an organization's method for utilizing information, digital services and associated technology.

Professionals in IT governance are responsible for ensuring availability of digital services, service levels, and service quality which satisfy short-term and long-term business needs. They establish operating policies and practices which conform to extant national, regional and international regulations while ensuring that the organization's IT investments are justified.

Project Management

Project management as it is named is about the management of projects. Therefore it's about those skills that are put to use for effective development and implementation of business processes to meet identified business needs. Project management tools or resources and skills are used in executing projects within agreed parameters of cost, time-scale, and quality.

IT Management

This skills category refers to the management of the IT infrastructure and every resource required for planning, developing, supporting and delivering IT services and products to meet the strategic goals of a business. It is responsible for preparing, implementing and managing new or modified services; and the supervision and maintenance of regulatory, legal and professional standards. Also, systems performance and service quality are managed to evaluate their overall contribution to business performance, their financial costs and sustainability. IT management maintains oversight over third-party services purchased by the organization and ensures development of continual service improvement plans so that the IT infrastructure adequately supports business.

Information Security

This is a specialty skills category with focus on the capacity to select, design, justify, implement and apply relevant controls and management strategies to maintain the security, confidentiality, integrity, availability, and accountability of information systems as well as maintain strict adherence to relevant legislations, regulations and standards. This is accomplished using a combination of hardware and software IT infrastructures. Career paths include certification tracks concerned with Computer security, IT Security, Network Security, Server Administration, and System Administration.

18

Key ICT Certifications and their Relevance

We shall be looking at some in-demand certifications in this section in terms of their course titles, credential owner-vendors and their industry relevance. We shall also see how some of them follow vendor designed certification paths an interested candidate may take to achieve a firm career footing in the ICT industry.

Understand also that IT certifications are of two classes; *Vendor-specific* and *Vendor-neutral* certifications. Vendor-specific certifications are those certification courses or programs which their credentials originate from and are administered by a specific ICT organization with particular focus on skills and knowledge about their proprietary products or technologies. Vendor-neutral certifications on the other hand deals with skills and knowledge originating from and administered by the technology industries' global standards associations and knowledge bodies and not one specific ICT organization's product, technology or specification. Therefore, they validate cross-cutting skills and knowledge applicable to various vendors' platform products or technologies.

Vendor-neutral certifications

ITIL Certifications

ITIL which stands for Information Technology Infrastructure Library was published by the United Kingdom's Central Communications and Telecommunications Agency (CCTA) and has primary publications in the areas of Service Strategy, Service Design, Service Transition, Service Operation and Continual Service Improvement. ITIL has been adopted worldwide and is being used by educators, certifiers, practitioners and companies.

It acts as a framework to help manage IT services and also help companies align their business and IT objectives[2].

ITIL, now owned and managed by AXELOS uses Accredited Training Organizations (ATOs) for training, and ITIL certification exams are administered at the end of a training program.

ITIL offers five different certification levels and uses a credit system all through its certification levels, whereby for each certification, one must earn a certain number of credits. In order to achieve ITIL Expert certification for instance, a candidate is required to earn a total of 22 credit units. The certification levels are as listed below;

- *ITIL Foundation*: Entry-level certification for those requiring basic ITIL frameworks understanding or understanding of how ITIL is used for IT service management in any organization with full ITIL adoption.
- *ITIL Practitioner*: The ITIL Practitioner is the newest entry to the ITIL certification scheme, with the exam offered for the first time in February 2016.
- *ITIL Intermediate*: The ITIL Intermediate consists of several modules each of which focuses on a different aspect of IT service management. A Module may be classified as a Service Lifecycle or Service Capability module.

The Service Lifecycle module includes:
- ✓ Service Strategy (SS)
- ✓ Service Design (SD)
- ✓ Service Transition (ST)
- ✓ Service Operation (SO)
- ✓ Continual Service Improvement (CSI)

The Service Capability module includes:
- ✓ Operational Support and Analysis (OSA)
- ✓ Planning, Protection and Optimization (PPO)
- ✓ Release, Control and Validation (RCV)
- ✓ Service Offerings and Agreements (SOA)

A candidate may achieve qualification by choosing a path specific to one module or by choosing courses from a mix of both modules. At least two years of IT service management experience and accredited training is required.

- *ITIL Expert*: This certification leads to better implementation of IT service management processes and best suited for those aspiring towards IT management roles, especially Chief Information Officers (CIOs) and Chief Technology Officers (CTOs).
- *ITIL Master*: This Apex certification is suited for Architects, planners, designers and IT consultants.

An ITIL certification has always been valued by large corporations who have full adoption of the ITIL framework as their IT standard. Small and medium-sized enterprises (SMEs) are also beginning to adopt the ITIL framework as well as demand for employees with ITIL certifications. ITIL certification is a valuable skill for every IT professional and job roles include Project Lead, Project Managers, Service Providers, System Administrators, IT support, IT Management, Chief Information Officers (CIOs), Chief Technology Officers (CTOs), IT audit managers, IT security managers, and IT consultants.

COBIT Certification

COBIT is an abbreviation for Control Objectives for Information and related Technology. It is a framework developed by ISACA for The Information Technology Governance Institute (ITGI) and addresses the issue of governance around IT. COBIT ensures that;

- IT is aligned with the business
- IT enables the business and maximizes benefits
- IT resources are used responsibly
- IT risks are managed

COBIT 5 which is the current version released in 2012 is used globally and has been particularly successful in the financial markets where auditing concepts are better understood[3].

ACM/IEEE Computer Science Curriculum

This is the Association for Computing Machinery (ACM) and the Institute for Electrical and Electronic Engineers (IEEE). It is in use by colleges and educators in North America, Europe, Australia and New Zealand. More information can be found at *http://www.acm.org/* and *http://www.computer.org/*.

CMMI®

This stands for Capability Maturity Model Integrated developed by the Software Engineering Institute (SEI) at Carnegie Mellon University, Pittsburgh, Pennsylvania. It is a process improvement maturity model that is focused on the development of products and services. It addresses the product life-cycle from concept through development and delivery and the maintenance phase[4]. More information can be found at http://www.sei.cmu.edu

PRINCE2 Certification

The word PRINCE is derived from the phrase "**PR**ojects **IN** Controlled Environments". It is actually not an ICT or technology certification but essential when paired with IT management related certifications. Prince2 is used extensively in UK Government departments and now in-demand globally. It is widely used in industry and business. An excerpt from the website at:
http://www.ogc.gov.uk/methods_prince_2.asp states thus[5];
PRINCE2 is a generic sometimes tailored, simple to follow project management method. It covers how to organize, manage and control your projects. It is aimed at enabling you to successfully deliver the right products, on time and within budget. As a Project manager you can apply the principles of PRINCE2 and the associated training to any type of project. It will help you to manage risk, control quality and change effectively, as well as make the most of challenging situations and opportunities that arise within a project.
A PRINCE2 project has the following characteristics:

- *Continued business justification*
- *Learning from experience*
- *Defined roles and responsibilities*
- *Managed by stages*
- *Managed by exception*
- *Focuses on products and their quality*
- *Tailored to suit the particular product environment*

PRINCE2 does not cover all aspects of project management. Areas such as leadership and people management skills, detailed coverage of project management tools and techniques are well covered by other existing and proven methods and are therefore excluded from PRINCE2. Prince2 documents best practices associated with project management and very much in-demand as additional certifications for those seeking to manage and lead ICT projects.

(ISC)2 Certifications

The International Information Systems Security Certification Consortium, Inc., (ISC)2 has a number of certifications on its related body of knowledge. Its body of knowledge is known as IT Security Essential Body of Knowledge, EBK. *"EBK is a collection of what US government IT security managers believe are the essential technology and management skills any IT staff should have to protect federal networks from cyber-attacks and unauthorized access[6]"*. The EBK is the US Department of Homeland Security and the US Government's version of the National Institute of Standards and Technology's (ISC)2.

The (ISC)2 Certification Program offers seven core security credentials:

- *Systems Security Certified Practitioner (SSCP)*
- *Certified Information Systems Security Professional (CISSP)*
- *Certified Authorization Professional (CAP)*
- *Certified Secure Software Lifecycle Professional (CSSLP)*
- *Certified Cyber Forensic Professional (CCFP)*

- *HealthCare Information Security and Privacy Practitioner (HCISPP)*
- *Certified Cloud Security Professional (CCSP)*

CISSP credential holders can further specialize and obtain the following certifications:

- *Information Systems Security Architecture Professional (CISSP-ISSAP)*
- *Information Systems Security Engineering Professional (CISSP-ISSEP)*
- *Information Systems Security Management Professional (CISSP-ISSMP)*

IT professionals who are not able to meet the work requirements can qualify for the associate of (ISC)2.

SSCP certification is the basic foundation credential for this certification track. Without requisite work experience, a candidate who achieves this certification would be issued the Associate of (ISC)2 credential. This same requirement holds true for CAP, CSSLP, CCFP, HCISSP, CCSP and CISSP exams. What is commonly done by SSCP holders is that they earn the CISSP; after which they specialize in any of security architecture (CISSP-ISSAP), security engineering (CISSP-ISSEP) or security management (CISSP-ISSMP).

To maintain this certification, an annual maintenance fee is required including achieving 15 continuing professional education (CPE) credits annually.

Entry-level Associate of (ISC)2 credential holders can be network administrators, systems administrators, security specialists or security consultants. However, with higher credentials like the CISSP, job roles such as security auditors, security managers, security analysts, security consultants, IT directors, chief information security officers (CISOs), and network architects are common.

Linux Certifications

Linux is an open source operating system. This means it is not a proprietary product and as such a vendor-neutral technology.

The Linux Professional Institute's certification program comprises of three certifications:

LPI Linux Essentials: This is the entry level exam for beginners. It is not a prerequisite towards the Linux administrator LPIC-1exam. Linux Essentials exam is designed to validate familiarity with the basics of the Linux operating system; ability to carry out file management, use the Linux CLI (Command Line Interface), perform backup and restore operations and write basic scripts.

Linux Administrator (LPIC-1): Also an entry-level certification and it validates the ability to install, configure and maintain a Linux workstation using the Linux CLI.

Linux Engineer (LPIC-2): This is a mid-level certification for network administrators of small and medium business networks.

Linux Enterprise Professional (LPIC-3): This certification is for higher-level Linux professionals and validates the ability to plan, design, implement and troubleshoot Linux installations in enterprise environments.

LPI certifications are administered by Pearson VUE. All LPI certifications are valid for five years.

Job roles include as system administrators, network administrators, system engineers and technical support specialists. Others are as cyber security engineers, cloud computing system administrators or even as technical education specialists.

PMI Certifications

Project Management Institute (PMI) certifications are not technology or ICT based certifications but are vendor-neutral IT relevant certifications which are essential for IT management roles. Any choice of each of the certifications can be made as none is a prerequisite for achieving the other. But one must be guided by what area of interest the certification addresses relative to the career path chosen. The various certifications are listed below. They are;

- *CAPM: Certified Associate in Project Management*
- *PMP: Project Management Professional*

- *PgMP: Program Management Professional*
- *PfMP: Portfolio Management Professional*
- *PMI-ACP: PMI Agile Certified Practitioner*
- *PMI-RMP: PMI Risk Management Professional*
- *PMI-SP: PMI Scheduling Professional*
- *PMI-PBA: PMI Professional In Business Analysis* [7]

The CAPM certification is valid for 5 years after which PMI requires candidates to re-certify to re-validate their credentials. The other credentials; PMP, PgMP, PfMP, PMI-ACP, PMI-SP and PMI-PBA are however valid for only 3 years after which a credential holder is expected to re-validate the certification.

Job roles commonly associated with holders of these credentials include as project managers or Project coordinators. Others may become business analysts or business managers.

EC-Council Certifications

The EC-Council's Career Path is segmented into skill levels; Fundamental, Intermediate, Advanced, Specialist and Expert levels. Their certifications are highly valued in the field of computer security.

Entry into this security specialty can begin with the entry-level EC-Council Certified Secure Computer User (CSCU) certification, and later graduate to the Certified Security Specialist (ECSS) credential. Next on the ladder is the Certified Ethical Hacker (CEH) certification which is one of the highest valued IT security certification. The EC-Council's Certified Network Defender (CND) certification validates the ability to install, configure, manage and maintain an organization's security infrastructure, including firewalls, endpoint security, intrusion detection and other security protection technologies. The EC-Council's Incident Handler (ECIH) credential however, validates the skills for handling security breaches in real time; analysis, diagnosis, and identification with recommendations for their mitigation.

The CEH is the EC-Council's core certification for more advanced or specialized certifications. CEH certified professionals utilize the same knowledge and tools malicious hackers deploy, but in a legitimate way for detecting weaknesses and vulnerabilities in computer systems security. For instance to become a penetration tester, a candidate must achieve the EC-Council Certified Security Analyst (ECSA) track before taking Licensed Penetration Tester (LPT) certifications.

EC-Council security certifications include the following[8];

- *Certified Security Computer User (CSCU)*
- *Certified Network Defender (CND)*
- *Certified Ethical Hacker (CEH)*
- *EC-Council Certified Security Analyst (ECSA)*
- *Licensed Penetration Tester (LPT)*
- *Computer Hacking Forensic Investigator (CHFI)*
- *EC-Council Disaster Recovery Professional (EDRP)*
- *EC-Council Certified Incident Handler (ECIH)*
- *EC-Council Certified Encryption Specialist (ECES)*
- *EC-Council Certified Security Specialist (ECSS)*
- *Certified Network Defense Architect (CNDA)*: Available only through some specific government agencies and candidate must possess the CEH certification.
- *Certified Chief Information Security Officer (CCISO)*: Five years information security and management experience in each of the CISO domains is a requirement for taking this certification exam. It is an essential certification targeted for chief security officers.

The job outlook for EC-Council certifications looks great with a variety of job portfolios lined up. The job roles EC-Council's credentials fit into are ethical hacking (CEH), encryption (ECES), security analysis (ECSA), forensics (CHFI) and Penetration testing (LPT). A holder of these credentials would also do well as a security consultant to various multinational organizations.

EC-Council certifications are well recognized and respected in the ICT industry and recommends their official training before attempting any of its certification exams. Candidates who go for other training options instead of their official training program must complete an eligibility form, provide proof of a minimum work experience and pay a fee of $100. Prometric and Pearson VUE testing centers administer their exams while EC-Council's online Exam Portal also provides an alternative platform for testing. For further information on specific certification tracks of interest, visit their website.

CompTIA Certifications

CompTIA's certification programs are one of the most popular IT industry certifications. CompTIA like others classifies their certifications based on four IT skill levels; Foundational, Professional, Master and Specialty skill levels.

CompTIA's Professional level certifications cover a wide range of IT areas of expertise such as security, networking, cloud computing, server administration, Linux administration, project management and so on with nine (9) certification tracks. In the "Specialty" class are four (4) certification tracks while "Foundational" and "Master" Skill levels have one certification each. There are also certifications for document imaging, cloud essentials, healthcare IT and IT trainers. Below is a list of all the globally recognized CompTIA IT certifications[9];

- *CompTIA IT Fundamentals*
- *CompTIA A+*
- *CompTIA Network+*
- *CompTIA Cyber Security Analyst (CSA+)*
- *CompTIA Security+*
- *CompTIA Linux+*
- *CompTIA Cloud+*
- *CompTIA Mobility+*
- *CompTIA Server+*
- *CompTIA Project+*
- *CompTIA Advanced Security Practitioner (CASP)*
- *CompTIA CDIA+*
- *CompTIA Cloud Essentials*

- *CompTIA Healthcare IT Technician*
- *CompTIA CTT+*

CompTIA makes it easy for entrants to decide on a career path by classifying these certifications into skill area categories which serves as career paths. Therefore there are Information security; Network and cloud technologies; Hardware, services and infrastructure; IT management and strategy; Web and mobile; Software development; Training and Office productivity certification paths to choose from.

If you visit CompTIA website, the "Certifications" page offers choices for a desired certification level and career path. When you make a selection, the page returns a list of certifications according your choices. If you are interested for instance in information security, the path would include IT Fundamentals, A+, CSA+, Network+, Security+, and CASP. CompTIA credentials are a gateway to a variety of job roles depending on a professional's experience level, skill level and area of interest.

Job roles applicable include network, system or security administrators, security managers, specialists or administrators, and security consultants. Others are storage and server administrators, server support, and server technicians; Linux database administrators, network administrators or web administrators; cloud specialists, developers or system and network administrators; support administrators, support technicians or support specialists; security engineers, cyber security analysts or specialists, threat or vulnerability analysts and so on all according to the certification tracks achieved by CompTIA credential holders.

ISACA Certifications

When you talk about information systems auditors, risk management and IT governance professionals and managers, ISACA's certifications come to mind. ISACA's major certifications satisfy the American National Standards Institute (ANSI) accreditation as having met ISO/IEC 17024 standards which stipulates General Requirements for Bodies Operating Certification Systems of Persons. The core certifications they offer and administer are[10];

- *CISA: Certified Information Systems Auditor*
- *CISM: Certified Information Security Manager*
- *CGEIT: Certified in the Governance of Enterprise IT*
- *CRISC: Certified in Risk and Information Systems Control*
- *Cybersecurity Nexus and*
- *CSX Practitioner (CSX-P) Certification (New)*

The CSX Practitioner (CSX-P) is a new addition targeted at security practitioners who plan, respond and manage security incidents. There are five (5) security incident handling and response IT domains covered by the CSX-P certification namely;

i. Identify
ii. Protect
iii. Detect
iv. Respond
v. Recover

Job roles usually satisfied by CISA, CISM, CGEIT and CRISC credential holders include the job of security auditor, security management roles, and senior executive-level jobs like IT governance, chief information security officers or chief risk assurance officers, chief information officer (CIO) or chief technology officer (CTOs). Others are titles such as enterprise architects or security operations center analysts, security engineers, security architects or senior information technology auditor. The CSX-P confers individuals the recognition, ability and skills to work in such roles as security analysts, senior security analysts, incident responders, incident handlers, security managers or security consultants.

SAS Certifications

SAS IT certifications are focused towards business intelligence applications in the area of data analytics, data mining, data warehousing, data management, administration and programming.

The SAS Global Certification Program currently offers 13 credentials belonging to 5 skill categories namely[11]:

Foundation Tools:

- *SAS Certified Base Programmer for SAS 9*: Learn how to carry out database queries, analysis; how to import and export raw data files, manipulate data, combine SAS data sets and create reports.

- *SAS Certified Advanced Programmer for SAS 9*: Develop coding skills; interpret SAS SQL code, write SAS macros and provide software solutions.

- *SAS Certified Clinical Trials Programmer Using SAS 9*: Develop skills exclusively for working with clinical trials data, transforming raw data into polished, validated reports.

Advanced Analytics:

- *SAS Certified Data Scientist Using SAS 9*: For SAS Data Scientists who deploy SAS solutions.

- *SAS Certified Advanced Analytics Professional Using SAS 9*: Big data analytics certification.

- *SAS Certified Predictive Modeler Using SAS Enterprise Miner 13*: Become certified to build and implement predictive models.

- *SAS Certified Statistical Business Analyst Using SAS 9 Regression and* Modeling: For statistical business analysts.

Business Intelligence and Analytics:

- *SAS Certified BI Content Developer for SAS 9*: This certification empowers professionals with skills to create, implement and customize SAS interface applications, data management and dashboard.

- *SAS Certified Visual Business Analyst Exploration and Design Using SAS Visual Analytics*: Learn about SAS Visual Analytics, Visual Analytics Explorer, and Visual

Analytics Designer to add, manipulate, explore data, and also create reports.

Data Management:

- *SAS Certified Big Data Professional Using SAS 9*: This credential is designed for professionals who conduct statistical analysis using SAS and open source data management tools.
- *SAS Certified Data Integration Developer for SAS 9*: Learn data analysis and reporting using SAS platform and identify the platform architecture for SAS Business Analytics.
- *SAS Certified Data Quality Steward for SAS 9*: Develop skills for using DataFlux Data Management Studio.

Administration:

- *SAS Certified Platform Administrator for SAS 9*: SAS Business Analytics installation, maintenance and support; manage user accounts, monitor system performance, implement security, backup and storage and so on.

SAS also offers six additional technical certifications targeted at SAS Partners. Job roles are according to skill levels and include such job titles as software analysts, content developers, programmers, data managers, data scientists, statisticians, technical analysts, and platforms administrator etcetera.

The Open Group Certifications

This is another vendor-neutral global IT industry consortium that boasts more than 500 member organizations from across the world, including giants like Oracle, Philips, IBM, Huawei and HPE[12]. The list of certification programs handed out to professionals is as enumerated below;

Open CITS (Open Certified IT Specialist) Program

The certification tracks under this program are classified according to skill levels;

- *Certified IT Specialist* (Level 1): Prepares candidates to work under supervision

- *Master Certified IT Specialist* (Level 2): Candidates are trained to function independently, lead and provide customer solutions.
- *Distinguished IT Specialist* (Level 3): Functions in a leadership position

Open CA (Open Certified Architect) Program
- Certified (Level 1): Works under supervision or assistance
- Master (Level 2): Functions independently and in a leadership position.
- Distinguished (Level 3): A level 3 distinguished certified architect leads and handles complex projects from planning, design and analysis to implementation. Holders of the "distinguished" certification can be Chief/Lead Architects, Enterprise Architects or IT Architects. The Open CA credential has two tracks namely the "IT Architecture" and the newer "Business Architecture" tracks.

Open Group ArchiMate Certification Program
- ArchiMate 2 (for individuals to be fluent in ArchiMate modeling language)
- ArchiMate 3 (for individuals to be fluent in ArchiMate modeling language)
- ArchiMate 2 (designed for tools to meet requirements to support ArchiMate modeling language)
- ArchiMate 3 (designed for tools to meet requirements to support ArchiMate modeling language).
- ArchiMate 2 has Foundation (Level 1) and Certified (Level 2) skill levels while ArchiMate 3 has Foundation (Level 1) and Practitioner (Level 2) skill levels.

TOGAF (The Open Group Architecture Framework) Certification Program
- TOGAF 9 Foundation: Covers basic concepts, terminology and core principles for using the TOGAF 9 framework.

- TOGAF 9 Certified: This is a combination of TOGAF 9 Foundation course content and the knowledge and skills for applying the TOGAF 9 framework to enterprise architecture projects. After taking the Open CA or Open CITS certification, next on the ladder could be TOGAF 9.

IT4IT Certification Program
- IT4IT Foundation: The IT4IT Foundation credential focuses on basic skills, including core principles, terminology and basic reference architecture concepts

Open FAIR Certification Program
This Open Group certification does not focus entirely on Information Technology.

SNIA Certifications

The Storage Networking Industry Association (SNIA) is a non-profit consortium of storage vendors whose mission is to educate and certify IT professionals with interests in storage networking arts and sciences careers[13]. The result is their vendor-neutral storage education and credentials programs. Take a look at them below;

- SNIA Certified Storage Professional (SCSP): This credential was introduced in 2016 as a replacement for the older SNIA powered CompTIA Storage+. SCSP is a professional-level certification which validates knowledge of storage protocols, disaster recovery methods and basic storage networking concepts. It is tailored towards IT professionals working as cloud administrators; network, data management and backup administrators; sales, systems engineers; storage analysts, and implementation specialists. To obtain the SCSP certification, candidates must sit and pass the Storage Networking Foundations Exam.
- *SNIA Certified Storage Engineer (SCSE)*: SCSE certification prepares candidates who monitor and configure storage networks, apply best practices and standards, and carry out backup and restore operations. With this certification, the

specialty skills for providing hands-on storage solutions and function as a professional storage engineer are acquired.

▪ *SNIA Certified Storage Architect (SCSA)*: This is an advanced level certification focused on in-depth storage networking theory and best practices. It focuses on design and implementation and follows ITIL frameworks and ITSM (IT Service Management) principles. To certify, a candidate must first pass the Foundations exam and the Storage Networking Assessment Planning and Design exam (S10-310) to earn the SCSA credential.

▪ *SNIA Certified Storage Networking Expert (SCSN-E)*: The SCSP, SCSE and SCSA are prerequisites for the SCSN-E exams. To earn the SCSN-E, candidates must choose and complete a minimum of two SNIA partner storage certifications. The partner storage certifications could be drawn from any of the following vendors; Cisco, Brocade, Dell, EMC, Hitachi, HP and NetApp.

▪ *SNIA Qualified Storage Sales Professional (SQSSP)*: This certification is designed for sales engineers.

SNIA exams are available through Prometric testing centers.

SANS GIAC certifications

The SANS Institute was founded in 1989 for the purpose of IT security and administration information education and training[14]. It is therefore vendor-neutral on its technologies. SANS created the Global Information Assurance Certification (GIAC) program in 1999 through which certifications are administered, ensuring that individuals meet IT security knowledge and skills standards. SANS certifications follow four skill levels of achievement as seen below[15];

▪ *Introductory Level*: For Security administration area of expertise, we have GIAC Information Security Fundamentals (GISF) and GIAC Global Industrial Cyber Security Professional (GICSP).

▪ *Intermediate Level*: The certifications under this level are GIAC Certified Forensics Examiner (GCFE); GIAC Information Security Professional (GISP); and GIAC Security Essentials Certification (GSEC) representing three areas of expertise namely Forensics, Management and Security administration respectively.

▪ *Advanced Level*: The certifications are GIAC Systems and Network Auditor (GSNA) and GIAC Certified Forensic Analyst (GCFA); GIAC Network Forensic Analyst (GNFA) and GIAC Advanced Smartphone Forensics (GASF); GIAC Law of Data Security & Investigations (GLEG) and GIAC Security Leadership Certification (GSLC). They all represent such areas of expertise as Audit, Forensics, Legal, Management, Security administration and Software security respectively.

Others corresponding to management, security administration and software security respectively are; GIAC Certified Project Manager Certification (GCPM), GIAC Certified Perimeter Protection Analyst (GPPA), GIAC Certified Intrusion Analyst (GCIA), GIAC Certified Incident Handler (GCIH), GIAC Certified UNIX Security Administrator (GCUX), GIAC Certified Windows Security Administrator (GCWN) and GIAC Certified Enterprise Defender (GCED); GIAC Certified Penetration Tester (GPEN), GIAC Web Application Penetration Tester (GWAPT), GIAC Mobile Device Security Analyst (GMOB), GIAC Critical Controls Certification (GCCC), GIAC Continuous Monitoring Certification (GMON), GIAC Python Coder (GPYC), GIAC Response and Industrial Defense (GRID) and GIAC Secure Software Programmer - .NET (GSSP-NET); GIAC Secure Software Programmer -Java (GSSP-JAVA), and GIAC Certified Web Application Defender (GWEB).

▪ *Expert Level*: The areas of expertise covered at this level are Forensics, GSE and Security administration. Their corresponding certifications are GIAC Reverse Engineering Malware (GREM), GIAC Security Expert (GSE), GIAC Assessing Wireless Networks (GAWN), and GIAC Exploit Researcher and Advanced Penetration Tester (GXPN) respectively.

There are no required prerequisites for any of GIAC certifications. A candidate may apply and sit for any GIAC exam of choice. Official Training is highly recommended and using SANS training courses serves the purpose. Although training fee may be high, SANS training courses are usually recommended for achieving GIAC certifications.

With GIAC certifications, expect to fit into job roles in IT security. GIAC credential holders usually work as security analysts or specialists, information security engineers, network security administrators, penetration testers, database administrators, developers, cyber security specialists, forensic specialists, and risk assessment managers. Also, most Security Operations Center (SOC) analysts, engineers and supervisors are GIAC credential holders.

* * *

As you can see from the foregoing list, the certification tracks and career paths are numerous just for non-vendor specific certifications alone. There are yet other non-vendor specific certifications like the Six Sigma certifications, Help Desk Institute (HDI) certifications and others which are not so popular or have been omitted in this review. Relevant and powerful as most of them are, most graduates, students and even professionals may not even be aware these certifications exist in the IT industry. This is the importance of having the right information. Without relevant information, career advancing competencies will not be gained and without these competencies, there will be skill gaps in the IT sector with unfulfilled career expectations for many especially in the developing countries. This is what this book is set out to accomplish.

We shall examine a few major vendor-specific certifications in the next sections below.

Vendor-specific Certifications

Check Point Certifications
Check Point is an Israeli multinational software and hardware provider for IT security, network security, endpoint security, mobile security, data security and security management[16]. Check Point uses Authorized Training Center (ATC) Partners

worldwide for providing continuing education services on their IT security products and like most Vendors, uses Pearson VUE as the certification exam testing institution. Some of their ATC's offer testing services, but many do not. Check Point has approximately 150 Authorized Training Centers and over 4000 examination sites globally although Pearson VUE exam sites are also authorized. Course materials are available from only Check Point ATC Partners (Authorized Training Centers). Check Point certifications are valid for two years from the examination date.

Acquiring Check Point certifications gives one expertise in the technology that secures the internet for all Fortune and Global 100 companies. The benefits of becoming Check Point certified includes the skills to support and sell Check Point products, 2-year expert access to their SecureKnowledge database and advanced product documentation[17]. Some of their certifications include the following;

- *Check Point Certified Security Administrator (CCSA) R80*: It is an essential certification for IT Administrators who manage daily operations of Check Point Security solutions. A three-day course covers everything you need to start-up, configure and manage daily operations of Check Point Security Gateway and Management Software Blades systems on the GAiA Operating system.
- *Check Point Certified Security Administrator (CCSA) R77.30*: This is an essential certification also for IT Administrators who manage daily operations of Check Point Security solutions.
- *Check Point Certified Security Expert (CCSE) R77.30*: This next level certification validates troubleshooting skills and the ability to maximize the performance of security networks. It involves an advanced three-day course which is focused on how to build, modify, deploy and troubleshoot Check Point Security Systems on the GAiA operating system. Hands-on lab exercises deals with how to debug firewall processes, optimize VPN performance and upgrade Management Servers. It is all about Security Engineering.

- *Check Point Managed Security Expert (CCMSE)*: This advanced certification demonstrates expertise in Multi-Domain Security Management with Virtual System Extension. It involves learning how to deploy the latest cyber-security solutions to defend and prevent today's evolving threats which includes threat prevention and Secure Web Gateway.
- *Check Point Certified Security Master (CCSM) R77.30*: This highest grade certification is for advanced use of time-saving commands to configure and troubleshoot Check Point Security Systems and involves learning how to manage virtualized security in high-end networks and advanced security optimization techniques.

For more information, visit their website.

Microsoft Certifications
Microsoft as a big industry player owns a large suite of certification paths for her various software products. Talking about relevance with constant changes in technology, Microsoft certification is as relevant today as it will continue to be in the near future with its dominance in the windows desktop application market. Earning a "Microsoft Certified" solution certification demonstrates the skills and expertise to implement core business and productivity solutions which organizations rely on using Microsoft technologies. Therefore any of the current and relevant Microsoft technology certifications in diverse expertise areas would accelerate one's career in ICT. Key certification levels are Associate, Expert and Master Levels.

For associate levels, there is Microsoft Certified Technologist (MCTS) which is specific to a Microsoft product and Microsoft Certified Solutions Associate (MCSA), valid for early stage job seekers meant for on-site and cloud-computing skills in any one of Microsoft's core platforms (Windows Server, SQL Server, Windows Client or Visual Studio). Then, there are expert level certifications like *Microsoft Certified IT Professional (MCITP)* and *Microsoft Certified Solutions Expert (MCSE)*; *Microsoft Certified Solutions Developer (MCSD)* all designed to validate specific core skills. The master-level certifications include *Microsoft Certified Architect (MCA)* for highest achieving IT professionals and *Microsoft Certified Solutions Master.*

Other in-demand certifications are *Microsoft Office Specialist (MOS), Microsoft Certified Trainer (MCT), Microsoft Certified Systems Engineer (MCSE)* and *Microsoft Technology Associate (MTA).* Note that each of these certifications is in a series with different exam codes covering specific technologies and years of relevance.

All of Microsoft Certification programs are categorized into 5 different areas of expertise namely; Applications (Office, Office 365 and Microsoft Dynamics certifications); Server (Windows Server, Exchange Server, SharePoint and Microsoft Azure certifications); Desktop (Windows devices certifications); Developer (Visual Studio, SharePoint, Applications and Microsoft Azure certifications); and Database (SQL Server certifications) technologies.

A summary of Microsoft certifications is listed below; to view the certifications under each of the 5 categorized areas of expertise, visit Microsoft certifications web pages. The certifications classes are;

- *Microsoft Technology Associate (MTA)*
- *Microsoft Certified Solutions Associate (MCSA)*
- *Microsoft Certified Solutions Expert (MCSE)*
- *Microsoft Certified Solutions Developer (MCSD)*
- *Microsoft Specialist*
- *Microsoft Office Specialist (MOS)* [18]

If you are interested in becoming a Microsoft certified educator or trainer, you may go for Microsoft Certified Trainer (MCT) or Microsoft Certified Educator (MCE) credentials.

Unlock your way into the IT industry by becoming a Microsoft Certified Professional. An MCP status is a breakthrough into IT given Microsoft's dominance in Windows desktop technologies which is pervasive. It also gives you access to certain Microsoft community benefits with a personal exams dashboard, MCP embossed certificates and transcripts, downloadable certification logos, promotional offers and so on. To qualify for MCP, pass any of the MCSA, MCSD, MCSE and Specialist certifications. MTA or MOS certifications are not prerequisites for either MCP status or any of those four. Visit Microsoft websites and select any of the certification codes for all further information.

Oracle Certifications
Another IT industry technology giant and certification vendor is Oracle. Having developed and still developing various technology products, Oracle certifications just like Oracle products are tailored towards various areas of expertise such as Oracle Applications, Oracle Database, Oracle Enterprise Management, Oracle Foundation, Oracle Industries, Java and Middleware, Operating Systems, Cloud infrastructure, Oracle IT systems and Oracle Virtualization. That is a handful – ten (10) technology specialty areas! One's chosen area of specialization therefore determines the certification path taken within specific vendor's technology platforms relevant to his or her career.

Oracle Certified Professionals, (OCP) is in high demand globally.

Other top Oracle in-demand certifications are;
Java SE 7 Programmer Certified Associate, Java SE 7 Programmer Certified Professional, Java SE 6 Programmer Certified Professional, Oracle Database SQL Certified Expert, Oracle PL/SQL Developer Certified Associate, Oracle Database 11g: Administrator Certified Associate, Oracle Database 11g: Administrator Certified Professional, Oracle Database 10g: Administrator Certified Associate, Oracle Database 10g: Administrator Certified Professional and Oracle Database 12c Administrator Certified Professional.

Like others, Oracle certifications follow a sequence of skill levels from junior associate to associate, professional, master, expert and then specialist. For details on the nature and requirements of each Oracle exam, visit the Oracle University website for more detailed information.

Oracle Applications Certifications
Oracle Certified Implementation Specialists or experts certifications are the skill levels for Oracle Applications certifications meant for those who implement Oracle's various application suites and they are many. There are several products; some examples include Oracle E-Business Suite, Hyperion, JD Edwards, EnterpriseOne and PeopleSoft. Each certification is tailored therefore to specific application software.

Oracle Cloud Certifications
Oracle cloud credentials validate the skills for deploying and administering software applications in the cloud. The cloud credentials are many with skill levels as Certification Implementation Specialists, professional level credentials, and even a "Developer" credential.

Oracle Database Certifications
Oracle's Database certifications are tailored to target people who develop, implement or administer Oracle databases. The program covers Database Application Development, MySQL and Oracle Database. Database certifications are rated with revision numbers and alphabets according to the changes made over the years on the database technology. So it will continue to change as older technologies give way for newer implementations. At the moment, there is Oracle 12c. When yours truly entered the Oracle database arena, it was 11g. As versions change, professionals are required to take update exams.

The certification skill levels under the database category are Associate (OCA), Professional (OCP), Master (OCM), Expert (OCE) and Specialist tracks.

- *Oracle Database 12c Certified Associate (OCA)*: One of the following SQL exams must be passed before the administration exam.
  - Oracle Database 12c SQL
  - Oracle Database 12c: SQL Fundamentals
  - Oracle Database 11g: SQL Fundamentals I
  - Oracle Database SQL Expert

The Oracle administration exam may either be Oracle Database 12c: Installation and Administration or Oracle Database 12c: Administration.

- *Oracle Database 12c Certified Professional (OCP)*: OCA Database 12c Administrator is a prerequisite for achieving this more advanced credential.
- *Oracle Database 12c Certified Master (OCM)*: OCP Database 12c Administrator certification is a prerequisite for achieving this credential.
- *Oracle Database 12c Certified Expert (OCE)*: OCP Database 12c or 11g Administrator credential is a prerequisite for this certification.

A candidate may certify as Data Guard Administrator, RAC and Grid Infrastructure Administrator or Performance Management and Tuning by passing one exam. To earn the Maximum Availability credential, one must pass both the RAC and Grid Infrastructure Administration and Data Guard Administration certifications.

Oracle Enterprise Management Certifications

- *Oracle Enterprise Manager Application Quality Management 11g Certified Implementation Specialist* certification professionals who implement Oracle's Application Quality Management solutions. One exam required. Check Oracle website.
- *The Oracle Enterprise Manager 12c (older 11g) Certified Implementation Specialist* for applications, databases, architecture, systems, reporting, installation and storage

Oracle Foundation Certifications

This requires passing just one exam;

- *Oracle IT Architecture Release 3 Certified Architecture Specialist*: Learn how to plan, design, develop, document and implement solutions with adequate products knowledge.
- *Project Lifecycle Management Certified Implementation Specialist*: Targeted at project managers who manage, implement and administer Oracle projects.

Oracle Industries Certifications

Oracle Industries references various Oracle software solutions for the retail, communications, health services; and insurance, tax and utilities industries. All certification tracks under this category are regarded as Certified Implementation Specialists for each Oracle industry product.

Oracle Java and Middleware Certifications

Java and Middleware credentials are available for Associate, Professional, Master, Expert and Specialist skill levels. The common job titles or roles are as Java Developer, Java Programmer, System Administrator, Architect and Implementation Specialist. Check out certifications options at the Oracle university website.

Oracle Operating Systems Certifications

Oracle certifies candidates on base Operating Systems used for the Oracle software environment. They are Linux and Solaris and it's strictly for administrators and Oracle implementation specialists. Oracle Linux certifications are six (6) in number while Solaris are about eleven (11). Visit their website for more information.

Oracle Systems Certifications

Oracle's Systems certifications include Engineered Systems such as Big Data Appliance, Exadata, Exalogic, Exalytics and Private Cloud; Servers such as Fujitsu and SPARC; and Storage like Oracle ZFS, Pillar Axiom, StorageTek, Sun Flash and Sun Storage. Visit the Oracle university certifications web page.

Oracle Virtualization Certifications

Oracle Certified Implementation Specialists certifications for Oracle Virtualization certifications cover Oracle Virtual Desktop Infrastructure and Oracle Virtual Machine (VM).

The enormous and wide technologies covered by Oracle makes Oracle credentials highly valuable. One needs to choose an area of specialization and focus on those certification tracks that would be of greatest benefits to companies running on Oracle Database, Oracle Cloud, Oracle Linux or Solaris, Oracle operating systems, enterprise management software and so on;

and they are many. Oracle is said to have more than 420,000 customers in 145 countries[19]!

Cisco Certifications

Cisco is another IT industry leader with varieties of certifications and certification paths; focus is on network infrastructure and support technologies. Cisco certifications are one of the most popular and duly recognized in the IT industry. Skill levels are graded from entry-level to associate, professional, specialist, expert and architect levels. Cisco certifications are tailored to satisfy primarily two career paths that correspond to Cisco technology products and services in two expertise areas namely *Network Design* and *Network Operation and Administration.* Cisco exams are available through Pearson Vue testing centers worldwide.

Below is a list of the relevant Cisco certifications, besides the specialist certification tracks;

- *Cisco Certified Entry Networking Technician (CCENT)*
- *Cisco Certified Technician (CCT)*
- *Cisco Certified Network Associate (CCNA).*

A candidate may begin from CCNA directly without taking the two-part entry level CCENT and CCT. Specializations include; CCNA Routing and Switching, CCNA Cloud, CCNA Collaboration, CCNA CyberOps, CCNA Data center, CCNA Security, CCNA industrial, CCNA Service Provider, CCNA Wireless. Associate certifications serve as prerequisites for equivalent CCNP or CCDP certifications.

- *Cisco Certified Design Associate (CCDA).*
- *Cisco Certified Network Professional (CCNP).* Specializations include; CCNP Cloud, CCNP Routing and Switching, CCNP Collaboration, CCNP Data center, CCNP Security, CCNP Service Provider, CCNP Wireless.
- *Cisco Certified Design Professional (CCDP)* - prerequisite is CCDA

- *Cisco Certified Internetwork Expert (CCIE).* Specializations are Collaboration, Data Center, Routing and Switching, Security, Service Provider and Wireless. CCIE and CCDE have no prerequisite certifications.
- *Cisco Certified Design Expert (CCDE).*
- *Cisco Certified Architect (CCAr).* [20]

Acquiring the CCAr certification places one at the highest level of all Cisco certifications. It has been regarded as equivalent to earning a doctorate degree and it is very difficult to achieve. Job roles include as Senior Network Engineers, Enterprise Architects, Data Center Architects, Network architects or Senior Network Infrastructure Architects. To achieve this certification, one must certify first as a CCDE, and then defend a business-case-scenario network design solution before a Cisco appointed board of examiners.

Looking at the above list, it is evident that one can follow the tracks from associate skill level along either the "Design" or "Network" career path. You can either be a CCNA or CCDA; depending on that, you could graduate to CCNP or CCDP; and next CCIE or CCDE! Depending also on your chosen career interests, you may decide to take any of the specialist options.

Cisco professionals are in high demand globally because Cisco gears run the largest chunk of the internet traffic globally. Therefore pursuing a career through Cisco certifications is a good bet on wider opportunities.

Associate level job roles include titles such as Network or Telecommunications Engineers, Network Technicians, Network Analysts, Network Operations Center Analysts or Technical Specialists. The professional level credentials are usually for Network administrators, Network Engineers or Senior Network Design Engineers, Senior Network Analysts or just Network Designers.

The experts include Network Architects, Team Lead Engineers, Systems Engineers, Senior Network Engineers or Senior Network Administrators.

Juniper Networks Certifications
A competing vendor in the network design, operation and administration products category is Juniper Networks. Their certification programs grade skill levels according to the order; associate, specialist, professional and expert. They cover specific areas of expertise in line with Juniper Networks' products and solutions. There are three certification tracks. Areas covered are Routing and Switching, Data Center, Junos Security, and Service Provider for Juniper Network Technology. The second track is for design while the third track is products and technology. Below is a summary[21];

JNCIA-Junos (Associate) is an entry level certification and a prerequisite for higher certification tracks.
JNCP Network Technology Tracks:
- JNCP Enterprise Routing and Switching: *Juniper Networks Certified Specialist Enterprise Routing and Switching (JNCIS-ENT), Juniper Networks Certified Professional Enterprise Routing and Switching (JNCIP-ENT), Juniper Networks Certified Expert Enterprise Routing and Switching (JNCIE-ENT)*
- Junos Security: *Juniper Networks Certified Specialist Security (JNCIS-SEC), Juniper Networks Certified Professional Security (JNCIP-SEC),* and *Juniper Networks Certified Expert Security (JNCIE-SEC)*
- Junos Service Provider Routing and Switching: *Juniper Networks Certified Internet Specialist (JNCIS-SP), Juniper Networks Certified Internet Professional (JNCIP-SP),* and *Juniper Networks Certified Internet Expert (JNCIE-SP)*
- Junos Data Center: There are two certifications here although one can take one exam; the *Juniper Networks Certified Professional Data Center (JNCIP-DC)* and the Expert-level (JNCIE-DC) certification. *Juniper Networks Certified Specialist Enterprise Routing and Switching (JNCIS-ENT)* is a prerequisite for JNCIE-DC certification.
JNCP Design Tracks: JNCDA is a prerequisite for all.

- Data Center Design: *Juniper Networks Certified Design Associate (JNCDA), Juniper Networks Certified Design Specialist, Data Center (JNCDS-DC)*
- WAN Design: *Juniper Network Certified Design Specialist, WAN (JNCDS-WAN)*
- Security Design: *Juniper Network Certified Design Specialist, Security (JNCDS-SEC)*

JNCP Product and Technology Tracks: No prerequisite

- Firewall/VPN: *Juniper Networks Certified Specialist FWV (JNCIS-FWV)*
- QFabric: *Juniper Networks Certified Specialist QFabric (JNCIS-QF)* – Prerequisite is JNCIS-ENT
- SDN and Automation: *Juniper Networks Certified Specialist SDN and Automation (JNCIS-SDNA.* Prerequisite is JNCIA-Junos.

Juniper Networks' routing and switching gears are also commonly used in most ICT organizations; sometimes seamlessly implemented and other times mixed with Cisco or other enterprise gears although it is usually not a recommended practice. In some situations, it may be due to budget considerations. But overall, they are great products. So, job roles exist in the same classes and categories as listed under Cisco for JNCP credential holders, with some consulting firms who support Juniper products or ICT organizations specifically stating JNCP certifications as a requirement.

HP Certifications
If you are looking to work or already in organizations that support HP products and solutions, then you should consider HP's large collection of certification credentials in big data, cloud computing, networking, security, storage, IT management and more. HP certifications (now HPE) skill levels are categorized into four levels namely;

- *Foundation*: HPE Product Certified
- *Professional*: HPE Accredited Technical Professional (HPE ATP)

- *Expert:* HPE Accredited Solutions Expert (HPE ASE)
- *Master:* HPE Master Accredited Solutions Expert (Master ASE)

Below is a list of HPE certifications grouped according to the various areas of expertise as found on hpe.com certifications portal. Therefore one can choose from any of the following;

Big Data Certifications: HPE's big data credentials include:
- *HP ATP - Data Protector v9*
- *HP ASE- IDOL v10*
- *HP ATP - IDOL Server v10*
- *HP ASE - Records Manager Administrator v8*
- *HP ATP - Records Manager v8.x*
- *HP ATP - Structured Data Manager v7*
- *HP ASE - Vertica Big Data Solutions Administrator V1*

Data Center and Cloud Certifications
The certifications in the Data Center Cloud portfolio include:
- *HPE ASE - Data Center and Cloud Architect V3*
- *HPE ATP - Data Center and Cloud V2*

Networking Certifications
The certifications in this portfolio include:
- *HPE Master ASE - FlexNetwork Solutions V2*
- *HP ASE - FlexNetwork Architect V2*
- *HP ASE - FlexNetwork Integrator V1*
- *HP ATP - FlexNetwork Solutions V3*
- *HP APS - Networking (2010)*
- *HPE ASE - Data Center Network Architect V1*
- *HPE ASE - Data Center Network Integrator V1*

Operating Systems Certifications
The OS certifications include:
- *HP ASE - HP-UX 11i v3 Administrator V1*
- *HP ATP - HP-UX 11i v3 Administrator V1*

Security Certifications
- ArcSight:
- *HP Master ASE - ArcSight Security V2*
- *HP ASE - ArcSight Administrator v1*

- *HP ASE - ArcSight Analyst V1*
- *AP ASE - ArcSight Logger V1*
- *HP ATP - ArcSight Security V1*

Fortify:
- *HP ASE - Fortify Security V1*
- *HP ATP - Fortify Security V1*

SecureData:
- *HPE ATP - Data Security V1*

Server Certifications
Server certifications include the following;
- *Master ASE - Advanced Server Solutions Architect V3*
- *HPE ASE - ProLiant Server Solutions Integrator V3*
- *HPE ASE - Server Solutions Architect v3*
- *HPE ATP - Server Solutions V3*
- *HPE Product Certified - Converged Solutions (2017)*
- *HPE Product Certified - OneView [2016]*
- *HPE Product Certified - Synergy Solutions (2016)*

Storage Certifications
Storage certifications include the following;
- *HPE Master ASE - Storage Solutions Architect V2*
- *HPE ASE - Storage Solutions Architect V2*
- *HPE ATP - Storage Solutions V2*
- *HPE Product Certified - OneView (2016)* [22]

Citrix Certifications
We already discussed Citrix as one of the major ICT organizations in a previous section. Virtualization is one hot area of expertise in today's business world and Citrix's platform is used as a base platform by many cloud computing organizations which makes Citrix cloud computing technology a highly sought after resource globally[23]. Currently, over 400, 000 client organizations with more than a hundred million user base is said to be on Citrix products' subscription[24].

Citrix's enterprise XenDesktop, XenApp and XenServer and XenMobile are commonly deployed technologies. There is also NetScaler and ShareFile. If you are looking to gain recognition and expertise with a very high pay check (above $100, 000 per annum) in the IT domain, then becoming a *Citrix Certified Professional: Virtualization*, as well as other Citrix specialty certifications will do.

Citrix certifications are scaled on three skill levels; associate, professional and expert levels and are tailored towards App and Desktop Virtualization, Enterprise Mobility Management and Networking. Each level is a prerequisite for higher certifications, and each credential valid for three (3) years.

Below are other Citrix certifications:

- *Citrix Certified Associate: Virtualization (CCA-V)* – Prepares candidates to manage, maintain, monitor and troubleshoot XenDesktop 7.6 solutions.
- *Citrix Certified Professional: Virtualization (CCP-V)* – This level of certification prepares professionals to install, configure, scale, test and deploy XenDesktop 7.6 solutions.
- *Citrix Certified Expert: Virtualization (CCE-V)* – The Citrix expert level prepares candidates to learn how to design and document infrastructure, including security infrastructure; designing integrated virtualization solutions, analyzing existing environments; conduct planning and risk assessments.
- *Citrix Certified Associate: Networking (CCA-N)* – This program is for building skills targeted at configuring, assessing and designing infrastructure for NetScaler implementations; and integration with third-party technology as well as every other feature for creating solutions.
- *Citrix Certified Professional: Networking (CCP-N)* - This skill level is for certifying network engineers or candidates with a little networking experience who wish to develop advanced networking skills especially to implement, manage and optimize Citrix NetScaler.
- *Citrix NetScaler SD-WAN Certified (CC-SDWAN)* – Citrix newest addition which is tailored to prepares those who configure and manage the NetScaler SD-WAN technology for various clients.
- *Citrix Certified Professional: Mobility*

(CCP-M) - is targeted at mobile designers and developers familiar with design, installation, configuration and administration of a Citrix XenMobile Enterprise solution. Mobile device management, mobile application management and secure productivity are also part of this course.
More information is available on the Citrix official website.

AWS (Amazon Web Services) Certifications
Amazon Web Services is one of the current trending cloud focused high in-demand IT certification of the moment. Their certification program grades skill levels from associate to professional; and then specialty certifications.

The associate level is an entry-level certification point and demonstrates competencies in designing and deploying scalable systems on AWS. There is a high market demand for certified AWS solutions architects. According to Computerworld, cloud computing technology ranks second only to security, as the place where organizations are increasing their IT budgets. Therefore AWS certified architects are highly valued to deploy and manage AWS solutions. According to 2017 salary survey by Global Knowledge, holders of any of each of the AWS certifications earn average $100,000 per annum (with combined reported average of about $125,591)[25].

The following are AWS list of certifications classified under roles as Architects, Developers and operations;
Architects
 - Associate: *AWS Certified Solutions Architect*
 - Professional: *AWS Certified Solutions Architect*
Developers
 - Associate: *AWS Certified Developer*
 - Professional: *AWS Certified DevOps Engineer*
Operations
 - Associate: *AWS Certified SysOps Administrator*
 - Professional: *AWS Certified DevOps Engineer*
There are two specialty certifications in Networking; *AWS Certified Advanced Networking* and Big Data; *AWS Certified Big*

Data. To earn a specialty certification, one must first earn an associate or professional certification.

If you are to go for AWS certification, it is recommended to have at least 6-months hands-on experience with AWS platform in order to get certified. For more information and registration, visit their website.

VMware Certifications

Just like Amazon Web Services and Citrix are popular on cloud computing globally, VMware is one of the largest known virtualization vendors, now a subsidiary of Dell Technologies[27]. The original VMware Certified Professional (VCP) certification has been broken into diverse specialty areas. VMware Certified Associate (VCA) is now the entry-level certification. One of the hottest specializations among the VCP tracks is VCP Datacenter virtualization (VCP-DCV current version VCP6-DCV) which validates skills, knowledge and capacity to perform basic deployment and administration of VMware's vCenter and ESXi.

VMware solutions help organizations streamline their various desktop, server, cloud and mobile IT infrastructure operations. Therefore, there is a high demand for VMware certified professionals especially in organizations running virtualized enterprise servers.

Some other main VMware products are VMware Horizon, vSAN, vCloud and vRealize Suite.

Industry reported average salary is around $102,962 according to Global Knowledge[28].

VMware offers certifications like most IT vendors at different skill levels and specific to areas of expertise their products are categorized. The professional certifications are listed below;

- *VMware Certified Associate (VCA)*
- *VMware Certified Professional (VCP)*
- *VMware Certified Advanced Professional (VCAP)*
- *VMware Certified Implementation Expert (VCIX)*
- *VMware Certified Design Expert (VCDX)*

The various certifications grouped under their respective areas of expertise are summarized below;

Cloud Management and Automation (CMA)

- *VMware Certified Associate 6-Cloud Management and Automation (VCA6-CMA)*
- *VMware Certified Associate 6-Hybrid Cloud (VCA6-HC)*
- *VMware Certified Professional 6-Cloud Management and Automation (VCP6-CMA)*; There is version 7 (VCP7-CMA)
- *VMware Certified Advanced Professional 6 – Cloud Management and Automation Design (VCAP6-CMA Design)*
- *VMware Certified Advanced Professional 6 – Cloud Management and Automation Deployment (VCAP6-CMA Deploy)*
- *VMware Certified Implementation Expert 6 – Cloud Management and Automation (VCIX6-CMA).*

VMware recommends two years work experience for each credential; both types of credentials above requires the VCP6-CMA as a prerequisite. Candidates who possess other VCP credentials or are seeking to upgrade to latest versions of the credential should check the certification page for current requirements.

Data Center Virtualization (DCV)

- *VMware Certified Associate 6: Data Center Virtualization (VCA6-DCV)*
- *VMware Certified Professional 6: Data Center Virtualization (VCP6-DCV)*
- *VMware Certified **Advanced** Professional 6: Data Center Virtualization Deployment (VCAP6-DCV Deploy)*
- *VMware Certified **Advanced** Professional 6: Data Center Virtualization Design (VCAP6-DCV Design)*
- *VMware Certified Implementation Expert 6: Data Center Virtualization (VCIX6-DCV)*
- *VMware Certified Design Expert 6: Data Center Virtualization (VCDX6-DCV)*

vSphere, VMware's infrastructure software suite is the base technology around which the data center certifications are built to validate individuals at various skill levels for installing, configuring, implementing and administering the vSphere data center operations and cloud environments. vSphere helps organizations streamline, gain insight and improve performance, availability and operations management of their IT infrastructure and applications. The suite has undergone (and would continue to undergo) several revisions with current versions at 6, latest vSphere 7.

Desktop and Mobility (DTM)

- *VMware Certified Associate 6: Desktop and Mobility (VCA6-DTM)*
- *VMware Certified Professional 6: Desktop and Mobility (VCP6-DTM)*
- *VMware Certified Advanced Professional 6: Desktop and Mobility Design (VCA6-DTM Design)*
- *VMware Certified Advanced Professional 6: Desktop and Mobility Deployment (VCAP6-DTM Deploy)*
- *VMware Certified Implementation Expert 6: Desktop and Mobility (VCIX6-DTM)*

VMware's two major products for which the above-listed credentials are focused are vSphere and Horizon with View.

Network Virtualization (NV)

- *VMware Certified Associate 6: Network Virtualization (VCA6-NV)*
- *VMware Certified Professional 6: Network Virtualization (VCP6-NV)*
- *Certified Advanced Professional 6: Network Virtualization Deployment (VCAP6-NV Deploy)*
- *VMware Certified Implementation Expert 6: Network Virtualization (VCIX6-NV)*

For more information on VMware education, certification requirements (like prerequisites) and training, visit; http://mylearn.vmware.com/portals/certification/.

With VMware certifications, one can work as a System Engineer, Network Engineer, or Cloud administrator and System Administrator roles.

SAP Certifications

Another big Enterprise Business Software vendor in the IT industry is SAP, a German global software company. When you hear about CRM (Customer Relationship Management), ERP (Enterprise Resource Planning), and SRM (Supplier Relationship Management) as well as other Enterprise-class software suites, SAP is one of the leading suppliers of these categories of products with a global clientele of over 345, 000 and counting[29].

SAP Certifications are rated at associate, specialist or professional skill-levels. The associate skill level is designed for entry level candidates new to SAP technology; the specialist credential is for validating skills in specific technology components and candidates are required to earn the associate skill level credential as a prerequisite while the professional skill level validates advanced, in-depth experience using SAP technologies. No prerequisite is required for the associate and professional level credentials.

Note that once you earn a SAP credential, there is neither expiry date nor a recertification requirement. The credential may only be outdated due to new technologies developed by SAP and introduced into their products and certifications. They administer Beta exams which credential holders take from time to time to keep their credentials up to date. Pearson Vue and official SAP Training centers conduct SAP exams. For cheaper bargains, I would recommend exploring the SAP "Certification in the cloud" program which is subscription based.

SAP certifications are categorized according to available SAP solutions. This is a convenient way of making SAP training and certifications choices easier to be matched to job roles and skills area by intending professionals. There are 14 solution categories, each category having its own list of associate, professional and specialist level certifications. The solution categories found on their website's certification portal[30];

- SAP Ariba Procure-to-Pay (P2P)
- SAP Business One
- SAP Business Objects
- SAP Customer Relationship Management
- SAP Enterprise Resource Planning
- SAP HANA
- SAP NetWeaver
- SAP Product Lifecycle Management
- SAP Solution Manager
- SAP Supplier Relationship Management
- SAP Supply Chain Management
- SAP Sybase Adaptive Server Enterprise (SAP Sybase ASE)
- SAP Enterprise Mobility Solutions
- SAP Industry Solutions

All current certification exams are listed on their "Training and Certification Shop" page. You will find a "List of Valid Exams", click on it and explore. Also, besides official SAP Training Centers worldwide, online training options are available through their various e-learning solutions like the SAP Learning Hub, SAP e-learning, SAP Live Access and SAP E-Academy. Check out which one or combinations that cater to your needs.

SAP is used by many multinationals that would be of interest to any career minded job seeker; therefore a SAP credential opens a lot of doors globally.

Salesforce Certifications
Sometimes, all a professional is looking for is an IT-enabled role-specific certification that can advance one's career. Salesforce credentials address specific organizational job roles from Architects to Administrators, App Builders, Consultants, Developers, Marketers, Specialists, and Pardot Experts.

To become Salesforce certified, a candidate can take proctored exams at a testing location or take online exams conveniently from home. Salesforce uses webassessor by Kryterion Global Testing Solutions for its certification administration. The following is a list of Salesforce certifications;

Architect Certifications

- *Salesforce Certified Technical Architect*
- *Salesforce Certified Application Architect*
- *Salesforce Certified System Architect*
- *Salesforce Certified Data Architecture and Management Designer*
- *Salesforce Certified Development Lifecycle and Deployment Designer*
- *Salesforce Certified Identity and Access Management Designer*
- *Salesforce Certified Integration Architecture Designer*
- *Salesforce Certified Mobile Solutions Architecture Designer*
- *Salesforce Certified Sharing and Visibility Designer*

Administrators Certifications

- *Salesforce Certified Administrator*
- *Salesforce Certified Advanced Administrator*

App Builder Certification

- *Salesforce Certified Platform App Builder*

Consultant Certifications

- *Salesforce Certified Sales Cloud Consultant*
- *Salesforce Certified Service Cloud Consultant*
- *Salesforce Certified Community Cloud Consultant*
- *Salesforce Certified Field Service Lightning Consultant*

Developer Certifications

- *Salesforce Certified Platform Developer I*
- *Salesforce Certified Platform Developer II*
- *Salesforce Certified Commerce Cloud Digital Developer*

Pardot Expert certifications

- *Salesforce Certified Pardot Specialist*
- *Salesforce Certified Pardot Consultant*

Specialists Certification

- *Salesforce Certified CPQ Specialist certification*

142

To understand further what any of these Salesforce credentials of interest is all about, summaries of the skill-sets these certifications validate for each job role-specific category are available at http://certification.salesforce.com.

Dell EMC (formerly EMC) Certifications

The Information technology trends in cloud, data, and storage are areas of expertise addressed by EMC's current certification tracks, streamlined with their business solutions in data storage; cloud computing, virtualization, data analytics, information security and other products that help organizations store, protect, manage and analyze data. EMC's business focus over many decades has been on computer storage hardware and software technologies[31]. The strength of their market dominance as the world's largest provider of data storage systems - with competitors like HPE, NetApp, and IBM and so on - resulted in the interest and acquisition by Dell now known as the merger – Dell EMC[32]. With this success, Dell EMC is now an IT conglomerate with a combined variety of relevant business portfolio consisting of Dell's enterprise server, personal computer, and mobile businesses together with EMC's enterprise storage business!

Therefore if you desire to become an industry recognized certified data storage engineer, architect, administrator, data scientist or developer and more especially on EMC's product line, EMC certification program is a sure bet.

EMC has a good market share in the storage industry sector, with their products and services widely used across myriads of data centers worldwide.

Each certification track in EMC's Proven Professional program is job profile and skill-area specific.

Summary of Dell EMC Proven Professional tracks available are:

- Associate
- Data Scientist (EMCDS)
- Cloud Architect (EMCCA)

- Cloud Administrator (EMCCAD)
- Implementation Engineer (EMCIE)
- Cloud Engineer (EMCCE)
- Storage Administrator (EMCSA)
- Technology Architect (EMCTA)
- Platform Engineer (EMCPE)
- Product/Technology specific

Dell EMC's VCE partner Certifications are;

- Associate
- Design Engineer
- Implementation Engineer
- Administration Engineer

All the certification exams under each Proven Professional and VCE certifications are listed on the Dell EMC certification page at; https://education.emc.com/content/emc/en-us/home/certification-overview.html. Visit the website for more information.

Informatica Certifications

Informatica is another industry player that has big business focus on data; big data, cloud computing, data management, data security, data center, data exchange, information life cycle management, data quality and data integration systems. Their solution technologies which aggregately form the toolsets used for establishing and maintaining data warehouses are integrated into their certification tracks to groom an army of certified professionals, who manage, deploy and implement the Informatica products for various clients. The Informatica client base is pegged at over 7, 000 client organizations with Microsoft and Salesforce ventures part owners of the company currently[33].

The skills categories and associated certifications are listed below;

PowerCenter Data Integration

- *Informatica Certified Specialist PowerCenter Data Integration Administrator 9.x*

- *Informatica Certified Specialist PowerCenter Data Integration Developer 10*

Data Quality
- *Informatica Certified Specialist Data Quality Administrator 9.x*
- *Informatica Certified Specialist Data Quality Developer 9.x*
- *Informatica Certified Specialist Data Quality Developer 10*

Master Data Management
- *Informatica Certified Specialist Master Data Management Developer*
- *Informatica Certified Specialist Master Data Management Administrator*

B2B Data Exchange
- *Informatica Certified Expert Data Integration 9.x: Velocity Methodology*
- *Informatica Certified Specialist, B2B Data Exchange: Developer*

Data Security
- *Informatica Certified Specialist ILM Data Archive 6.x: Developer*
- *Informatica Certified Specialist ILM Test Data Management: Developer*

Velocity
- *Informatica Certified Expert Data Integration 9.x: Velocity Methodology*

Big Data
- *Informatica Certified Specialist Big Data Management 10.1*

The inherent opportunities for job roles are many for Informatica certified professionals. Any data or information management and storage credential is positioned to tap into the demands of future IT requirements of organizations.

Free certification resources and further information can be found at http://www.webassessor.com/informatica. Register and create a test taker account to gain access to resources. Informatica has an online university which one may register as recommended in their skill set inventory document. The skill set inventory is a document you can freely download which provides sample exam questions, breakdown of topics and concepts, recommended training as well as the weight of exam questions for each topic and concept.

Cloudera Certifications

As pointed out earlier in this book about the trends in the ICT industry, big data is huge on the trend scale. One of the most important resource is data; therefore its acquisition, storage, analysis, security and management with cloud computing is of utmost importance to organizations of all sizes. Cloudera is also another company with big business focus on data and therefore own and manage credentials focused on big data for interested professionals. Cloudera's data scientist, data engineer, and Hadoop certifications provide clear paths to a career at the heart of information technology. Hadoop certification is among the top earning big data credentials in the industry.

Cloudera is a software company with software products and services built on the open source Apache Hadoop platform (an open-source framework used for distributed storage and dataset processing of big data using MapReduce programming model). Cloudera's importance is highlighted by the huge investments and partnerships with the company by giants like Oracle, HPE, Dell EMC, Intel, SAS, and Microsoft Azure announcing full support of Cloudera Enterprise[34].

If you want to play in the big league, here is an opportunity area to get certified.

Cloudera offers a range of certifications designed for professionals to develop and optimize skills in data analysis as well as develop, manage and administer Apache Hadoop systems. The following credentials for only associate and professional skill levels are offered for certification;

- *Cloudera Certified Associate Spark and Hadoop Developer (CCA Spark and Hadoop Developer)*
- *Cloudera Certified Associate Administrator* (CCA Administrator)
- *Cloudera Certified Associate Data Analyst* (CCA Data Analyst)
- *Cloudera Certified Professional Data Engineer* (CCP Data Engineer) – No prerequisite.

Cloudera certifications are only valid for 2 years. For more information, visit Cloudera University.

If your job involves or you love doing jobs related to preparing data for queries; using Query Language (QL) to analyze data; carrying out data analysis; workflow-oriented tasks like creating and reading HCatalog and Hive tables from HDFS data, or transferring data between internal clusters and external systems, then sign on and earn top salaries in the industry.

*   *   *

Actually it would have been a great pleasure to include all known certifications in the industry but that would be impractical for the scope of this book. The goal of this section of chapter four of this book is to highlight the very fact that certification is a key ingredient of continuing education; and alongside that, it carries market weight. Also, to make it easier for aspiring entrants to fully appreciate the value and depth of knowledge across multiple vendor-technologies certifications possess; and together with professionals already in the field of IT, to find a single repository from which an overview of a collection of top, relevant vendor and non-vendor credentials in the industry could be easily explored without the need for the strenuous, often confusing task of exploring the internet for such information.

Writing this chapter presented the most herculean challenge, researching and presenting this information although a handful are known to this author, having undergone this journey in IT to date and which by the way has no end in sight.

Some information are deliberately left out in some and provided in others for very obvious genuine reasons. With continual changes taking place within the industry's knowledge disciplines and technology, documenting some of them in a static publication would pass easily as misleading in terms of the status of such information with time. Therefore having provided established base information, it is rather more appropriate for each candidate, armed with a decision based on information gotten from this guide, to visit the vendor's or administrating body's website for each certification listed to gain more detailed information (little details like exam code numbers, prerequisites or if there are new requirements; new exam titles, course contents and retired exams) preparatory to taking the exams.

<u>19</u>

An Outsider's Guide into ICT Professionalism

Who is an "outsider"?
Contextually, an outsider here refers to someone who has no single academic or professional background in IT in any way but has a desire, interest, and keen commitment to learn in order to become part of the global community of IT technical and managerial professionals.

There are a few challenges for IT career lovers of all categories;

- The challenge of training for professional practice vs. training for certification exams.
- The challenge of choosing between sticking to one specific vendor's certification tracks and acquiring multiple vendors' credentials primarily focused on a chosen specialty area or multiple specialties.

These are genuine concerns and pose a challenge which demands deep considerations.

As for the first challenge, my view is that one should focus on both training objectives. Somehow, we have discussed in a previous section about the need to train with the goal of attaining technical proficiency as against the urgency to pass exams to achieve a certification credential for the sole purpose of using it as an advantage in getting hired.

Regarding the second challenge, oftentimes unforeseen circumstances around recruitment or employment just determine the career path taken by many people. But in practical terms, one should never leave critical career decision-factors to chance or accident in the long run. It is essential for someone to consciously make decisions from well determined goals while making choices in pursuit of a career

For some people, 'CV window dressing' (getting a certificate without adequate depth of knowledge and skills) does work out for them although they might be in a minority group but it's very likely that over time, such people are exposed as shallow frauds. Certification is not an exercise in erudition but is essentially meant to validate a possession of specialty skills and knowledge which can be readily applied practically in a specialty field.

In reality, attaining technical proficiency in knowledge concepts, theory and skills for an IT specialty is a far more guaranteed recipe for success in the exams. So it's a better win-win plan, far better than a 50-50 chance of success when one decides to take any available or perceived shortcut aimed only towards exam success.

An "outsider" therefore should be more concerned about gaining adequate understanding of the relevant technologies being studied and their real world applications. To succeed in this, the following action points should suffice;

✓ Decide from the section *"Certifications Skills Categories"* which ICT specialty group you would love to be a part of. There lies what you are passionate about.

✓ Next step is to revisit the section, *"Key Certifications and their Relevance"*. Carefully go through the lists – both vendor-specific and vendor-neutral – and match relevant certifications to your choice specialty group. Using a blank sheet of paper, do this for every vendor or non-vendor certification track except for those entirely not related to your chosen ICT skills category in the first step.

✓ Armed with your compiled list, rank the vendors – that is, rank the credential owners according to the following industry weight; client subscriber base, industry popularity, rarity of credential, and nature of ICT organizations that would demand holders of their certifications. Industry average salary scale may also be a factor as "value" ranking.

✓ Now you have an opportunity to make a decision by pruning this list; decide if it is vital for you to stick to one vendor certification track from associate to the highest skill level or to blend relevant tracks according to industry weight.

✓ Note: At entry level to ICT, it is important to focus on a single specialty area in your choice of credentials before diverging to other specialty tracks. If you start with database for instance, stick with it to gain entrance into the industry for starters before deviating to other specialties of interest. CVs with multiple divergent credentials without corresponding convincing years of experience in the associated job roles are usually looked upon with suspicion by hiring managers.

✓ After making a decision on what certifications and career path to follow, determine your preferred study and training modes (refer to the relevant section in this book where we discussed it). For instance, are you good with independent self-study?

✓ Get hold of every material resource necessary for achieving the credential you desire and begin your certification journey. I must suggest that you avoid any practice exam questions at this stage and focus strictly on learning the technology. I will say it again, use your imagination. For a fact, the training starts with you – your personal commitment - before considering any other training option you can afford.

✓ Whether your objective is to train, learn and validate your skills with a credential or train, learn and practice without necessarily sitting for a certification exam (especially for self-employed -private practice - professionals), train and study with a mindset towards writing certification examinations.

✓ Finally, no matter what your objectives are, try and gain access to virtual or physical practice labs and in the end attempt the exam, pass or fail.

20

ICT Testing Providers

Certification testing usually drives test-takers into registering with any one of the credential owners' testing providers' platform. In order not to find it confusing, let's learn a bit about three of the most popularly used testing providers one will encounter especially for new entrants to IT certification.

Pearson VUE™ is one of the most prominent testing providers in the world. While there are other testing providers around the world, Pearson VUE™, a part of Pearson Education remains the global leader in Computer Based Testing (CBT). Pearson VUE™ (Virtual University Education) implements state-of-the-art computer based testing (CBT) solutions that ensures that candidates demonstrate their knowledge, skills and commitment with utmost reliability and security for professional credential and certification programs globally.

According to their website, over 450 credential owners across the globe *"choose Pearson VUE to help develop, manage, deliver and grow their testing programs. From online practice tests to high stakes proctored exams that require the industry's most secure testing environments, Pearson VUE is the leader in computer-based testing — and much more"*[35].

Tests are delivered through a network of more than 200 company-owned and operated Pearson Professional Centers and more than 3,500 Pearson VUE™ Authorized Centers worldwide[36].

Pearson VUE's services for both test takers and the credential owners spread across almost every industry from the Academia and admissions, Financial and related services, Government, Health care, *Information technology (IT)*, Military to US licensing & global regulatory bodies[37].

Prometric Testing is another U.S. company involved in test administration globally. Prometric manages about three thousand testing centers in about 160 countries of the world. Prometric services cover areas like test development, test delivery, and data management.

According to their website, Prometric delivers and administers tests to approximately 500 client organizations in the academic, professional, government, corporate and *information technology* markets[38]. Prometric is particularly popular for its testing for the Graduate Record Examinations (GRE). Usually the testing provider decides the locations where a test is offered and as well, specific testing procedures for the day of the exam are dictated by the client.

Kryterion is a full-service test development and delivery company that provides world-class online testing technology integrating item banking, test delivery and real time reports. Kryterion is the market leader in live Online Proctoring, using internet connected remote webcam video monitoring that is connected to their certified proctors who observe test-takers during the test either at home, a learning environment, at work or anywhere. It is easy to use as long as you have a computer, a webcam and an internet connection.

Kryterion also has a global network of testing centers and partners and serves the Association, Technology and Education markets using its webassessor website. Among the various certifications we covered, some of them like Amazon AWS and

Informatica for instance use webassessor for their secure testing solutions.

For more information, visit their website.

Any one of these testing providers or combination of all for different certification exams of different vendors are likely to be used by a candidate. That determination is out of the control of the student as the credential owners determine which service proctors their exams.

"If you can't explain it simply, you don't understand it well enough"

~ Albert Einstein

Five

Starting and Building

A

Career in ICT

21

The Career Journey

As in every other profession in the world, there are no hard and fast rules to becoming an IT professional different from the usual routes and building blocks of a career in other fields. The traditional process that begins with education in the root foundational disciplines for ICT or through the foundational ICT disciplines is still essential and valid routes.

However, it is not necessarily cast in stone for ICT profession though it is required, to begin at the bottom and sequentially scale through those routes. The knowledge-driven information generation powered by ICT has made it easier for cross-functional knowledge and hence, roles across various disciplines with IT integration. In other words, some disciplines that were exclusive domains outside information technology are currently absorbed within IT systems, requiring either a dual competence in that discipline plus IT system skill or no more than competence in the IT system that serves that discipline is required; reason being that the IT system already compensates through embedded program codes for that discipline's knowledge-base.

What this means as regards the routes towards IT career professionalism is that someone's current status; academic or educational level and discipline, is not any more restrictive towards achieving IT professionalism. What is required is to IT-enable one's current status and grow into ICT from there.

John, an old friend of mine was just a diploma holder in accounting. With that qualification, he was struggling financially at a small firm where he worked. Sadly, he was laid off and another young chap took his position.

John as I knew him was someone who could be described as down to earth; not one to be laid off for negligence to duties. He is someone who takes seriously to everything he engages in; always seeking out ways to better his condition. As a matter of fact, John was on a part-time program to complete his Higher National Diploma (HND) in accounting at the time. His meticulousness led him to investigate why he was laid off as he found out that the new guy was also of the same academic qualification as him – at least he presumed so.

He said, "*I later found out that the new guy had and demonstrated higher level competence in SAGE Peach Tree accounting software. He had the certification and one other. I immediately stopped my loathing for him or anyone in the firm, but learnt a hard great lesson*". He knew that the firm was in the process of upgrading their operations and like others expected that they could have been nice enough by maybe allowing the older staff to catch-up through in-house training or get a heads up information at least. The firm however thought otherwise and that's the way the cookie crumbles most times.

The good news is that today, John with his background in accounting is a database specialist with a number of vendor certifications in his kitty – the ones I know of by the way. He currently is an employee of Oracle, West Africa.

How did an accountant become an IT Specialist? According to John, "*After that incident, luckily I was at the verge of writing my final HND exams. I had to concentrate fully on my studies, but my attention was being drawn to something else I had always ignored; the call to train by myriads of fliers, banners of small business training centers around the school environment. He* said, *"My journey truly began when I borrowed money to train informally at a small computer business center on Microsoft Office Suite – specifically MS Excel and MS Access. MS Access introduced me to my love for database systems!"*

Today, John is a multi-vendor certified professional and a specialist in Microsoft and Oracle products' technologies. He has his little 'small town' firm to thank for the wake-up call!

There are many 'Johns' out there today. Making that switch to ICT or simply consolidating your current position with a little information technology knowledge or skill is a starting point in this information generation.

My first book, *Mobile Phones and Tablets Repairs: A Complete Guide for Beginners and Professionals*[1] has helped discover and groom both technical and IT talents across the world; many of whom initially thought they had no flair or potential for technology. I receive testimonials from individuals and government, and also know many who were part of my organization's training programs (in IT, Electronics and Mobile Phone repairs) that I have monitored their growth.

One whose story I would like to share to conclude this section is a young man, Emeka also nicknamed, Smart. Smart completed his high school education and stayed back at home, telling his father he wanted to do business or nothing. I met his father through an associate of mine during a social function. His father suggested that he feared that his son would run into trouble soon and may even have started doing drugs as at the time. He was concerned and wanted him engaged even if just as an intern or one of my technical assistants. I had no need for new hands but when he, without my asking him, called at my office with the young lad, I took a liking to him. Somehow, looking back now I think I felt a handsome young man like that should not be left on the streets, wasting away. I cannot pinpoint exactly why I took him in because I usually declined such propositions except for those who attended my officially billed training events. So maybe it was just providence!

Naturally he could only fit in as an in-house apprentice in my computer/mobile phones support section. I also decided that it wouldn't hurt if he sometimes joined the team on IT consulting projects – particularly network engineering and satellite/VSAT installations projects. But Smart's interest was in mobile phone repairs and he became adept and efficient on the job. Under my supervision and guidance, he became a key person to our customers; level-headed and I began to suspect the old man played a fast one on me with his earlier claims about him being recalcitrant. I was happy all the same the way he turned out and the old man was grateful.

Smart was a good mentee and student and picked up very quickly working with the computer and using various software applications. He learnt and used several proprietary phone repair software and having caught up on internet research, suggested the acquisition of some tools we deployed in our work. I was impressed as he became an asset to the company and after a year was intermittently taking part in some of our large scale training consultancy services on youth empowerment. Before he was 2 years in my firm, his father as agreed, sponsored him to start-up his small business in mobile phones support which experienced tremendous growth.

Smart remained in touch with me, learning and growing. Through my encouragement, he secured admission to study computer engineering in the University while running his business with family members. According to him, *"I wanted to pursue a career in software engineering as a specialty, having seen the power of various proprietary vendors' phone software repair tools developed by others"*. I had advised him to begin his first degree in computer engineering as a background before specializing in software engineering in order to capture the entire broad knowledge in computer hardware. To cut this very long story short, this young man recently concluded his MSc. Software engineering from a university in the US.

Imagine if his hands remained folded, idle or his father did nothing. Some graduates even fold their arms and do nothing to stir up ambition within them. Without a push, there can be no breakthrough. Smart sponsored his education from that very venture which he was able to expand; his father was not a wealthy man as the entire family ended up depending on the success of that young man. Over time he was involved in premium smartphones sales, phone spare parts sales; mobile phones and computer accessories sales and support services and was travelling to Dubai, China on business trips while his younger brother whom he trained and others held fort running the business.

In life and business, the beginning is usually difficult but once one gets immersed in the process, the path gets clearer and opportunities open up. The mark of a champion is in his wounds. But many want to be champions without even a little scar.

How does one start and build a career in IT?

22

As An Aspiring Employee

Starting and building a career in IT for a new entrant yet to be gainfully employed is practicable though it may sound

unrealistic. From the moment someone sets out through desire to become part of the IT ecosystem, a career begins. Therefore, as an aspiring employee your career begins as soon as your studies and training kicks off!
Then;

Be Attuned

One must be mentally, emotionally and physically prepared to become a member of a group with common goals, world-view, skill sets and abilities to be relevant and valuable; and it must be done consciously!

Be Confident

Having prepared adequately through studies and training to become a useful asset to any organization that would need your services, be confident. Confidence is proof that you know your worth, your vocation and can define your value proposition to any potential employer as a problem solver. The basic function of any IT professional is to solve problems through technology.

Be Self-aware

If the skills and knowledge you possess are unknown to you such that you cannot clearly define how applicable they are in bringing about solutions to life and business problems, you are not ready! Be self-aware of the possibilities inherent in your abilities. With that you can make good deals for yourself when faced with a life changing opportunity. Knowing one's capabilities; its importance and usefulness is very empowering.

Communicate Effectively

If you know something, a true test to validate that knowledge is in your ability to communicate or explain it to someone else. For instance, if as an individual who holds credentials in data management or database administration you cannot summarily introduce yourself in a simple, clear language like this;

My name is John Doe. I am a computer scientist with specialist skills as a certified database administrator. I possess first-rate skills and knowledge of tools and platforms for capturing, analyzing, classifying, storing and managing data and other information assets of a business which are essential and strategic resource that helps management make decisions that are critical to overall business success...

Then you are not ready!

Create Good CV or Resume

A CV or resume is the first document through which a strong candidate for employment communicates what skills and abilities he or she possesses. There is a saying that one cannot give what one does not have. Therefore a good CV must have a soul and distinguishing qualities that sets one candidate apart from the others, even if they have similar qualifications. Do not create bland CVs; and you can't possibly do if you satisfy all the suggestions above.

Clean Up Your Digital Footprints

There's a merger between the physical and virtual world today. What previously were barriers to the human social and business network; the differences in the association of online profiles, behavior and character traits of an individual to the real-life physical attributes of that person, is now non-existent. We now live in a digital world where you must be mindful of the image your digital footprints cast about your personality to potential employers. Ensure therefore to setup clean profiles with good pictures in professional websites like LinkedIn. Facebook and Twitter are also great social media places where you can maintain a healthy online presence.

Understand that nowadays, before most hiring managers send out interview invitations, it may not be harmful practice for them to first take a peek online to form an impression of who you are. What would you want their impression of you to be?

23

In A Suitable Job Role

After you land a suitable job and role, and have become an employee of a choice firm, it is time to manage and grow your career vertically. Remember that if there's no alignment between an individual's personal values and aspirations with the company's values and aspirations, job performance would be below par.

Growing one's career does not depend on any one particular organization. Just as employees are expendable to employers when the need arises as is common nowadays, the same measure should apply to employers by employees should work conditions not be favorable to career growth. Always seek opportunities to grow your career by taking the following measures;

✓ Study immediately your growth potentials and career path within the firm and decide early if you intend to stay and grow in that organization for a life-long career pursuit or in the short run; that is, in terms of career-level, career determining factors and time frame you expect to make your exit for higher opportunities.

✓ Begin immediately to learn; acquire new skills and pursue continuing education credentials in line with your career goals.

✓ Imbibe sound, standard, ethical practice in your job and make it your signature work ethic.

✓ Be committed and invested in the job. No matter your decision; short-run or long-run, be a committed citizen of the organization and never be tempted to use organizational resources solely for your benefits. Overall, strike a balance between your need (valid) to manage your own career as well as your commitment to shared goals at your workplace; and if you exit, let it be with an excellent track record!

✓ Seek out within and outside the organization more experienced professionals; go under their mentorship and become part of their professional network. The best way to get your skills and face noticed is in networking and keeping in touch with the movers and shakers in your industry.

✓ Keep your eye on trends in the industry relative to your target expertise growth areas.

✓ Understand that while certifications may get you to and through the door (into the industry), growth into middle and senior management roles depend greatly on your academic qualifications first before certifications.

Also, focus on high utility, new specialist core credentials, being among the first few that achieve them.

✓ Study and understand the political power play and dynamics in your work environment. Every organization has a not-so-obvious web of connections and influence. I must emphasize here that should you decide early to grow on the long run in a particular organization, political skills more than your job expertise is the best determining factor for your overall job performance and growth, hence career success.

According to Daniel Goleman, political awareness skill as one of the emotional intelligence competencies helps one to *"accurately read power relationships, detect crucial social networks and accurately read organizational and external realities"*[2].

It is your ability to understand others with whom you share a working environment. More than intelligence and personal traits, research has shown that political skills best predicts one's career success either within upper or middle management roles or in lower level roles. Therefore politics in the office is very real and important for growth; but don't become too involved in it or become obsessed with politics rather increase your political intelligence quotient!

24

As A Self Employed (Private Practitioner)

One character trait I have observed about most entrepreneurs is that they love to be in control of events; especially as regards what they do, the impact and results of their best skills; their income, the direction their life is taking and what they are passionate about. Once it appears that these things are out of their control or under the control of other elements that manipulate these factors, indirectly controlling their life, frustration sets in.

Entrepreneurs need to be aware of, and control those things they are passionate about or they feel lost, bored and unproductive. They are not so good with routine jobs that are highly repetitive because that way, their best skills are not being expressed in their work.

Again, instead of deciding on a job by thinking in terms of such common considerations as salary, job position, city in which a job is in; an entrepreneur focuses on what gives him fulfillment first before rewards.

The question then is; are you cast in such a mould? If yes, then you may be better off self employed.

Joseph Jaworski said, *"Before you can lead others, before you can help others, you have to discover yourself"*[3]. While the qualities of an entrepreneur may lie within an individual from birth, people discover, grow into or are ready for it at different stages of life. Some people start earlier learning the ropes on the job – tough terrain; while others would have to first become employees to prepare – a journey of self-discovery. No one can say for sure, which route is best suited for success. For instance, billionaires like Microsoft's founders Bill Gates and his partner Paul Allen; Facebook's Mark Zuckerberg and many others were all basically students and not employees or ex-employees but went ahead to build great companies from scratch. Therefore there are both those that started and failed, and those that started and succeeded.

A few advantage former employees may have is track record and individual or client organizations with key people who already know their capabilities. However, it is not always the case that these advantages will work in one's favor when one decides to launch a startup firm.

A self employed IT professional is basically a consultant with expert skills used in exchange for financial benefits. In order to succeed, the following six success tips are recommended;

- ✓ Make yourself a more attractive commodity through a single focus specialist skill, not validated only by possessing a certification but an easily demonstrable problem-solving practice that businesses usually outsource.
- ✓ At startup stage, market yourself with offers that are almost free and for which personal cost to you are just your skills, time and energy.
- ✓ One limiting thought that holds back many who could do very well starting out on their own is capital and office rent. Money is important, especially for equipment and stationery. But your key capital is the knowledge and skills you possess; and you can start out using your home spaces. Most successful businesses started out from bedrooms, sitting rooms, dining tables, study, garages or makeshift spaces within their founders' home real estate. After your first or more deals, you move to an appropriate business location. Facebook for instance, started in Mark's room at Harvard and many others including yours truly's businesses, started from informal makeshift settings. You may be right if you say, it depends on the nature of business. But find an aspect of what you want to do among the skills you have and start from there.
- ✓ Consciously understand potential customer's needs and match them to your services and products. Exhibit a strong quality of service orientation, seeking out ways to increase

each customer's satisfaction and loyalty. Act as every client's trusted advisor.

✓ People often mistake entrepreneurship as an opportunity for excessive freedom. Lazy, undisciplined people cannot be successful entrepreneurs. It is more about flexibility than freedom. Make every time count (even when you exercise flexibility and allot time for leisure or winding down) as you invest in your pursuit round the clock; working, learning and then working some more.

✓ Expand. Get other specialists to join your team on a permanent or adhoc basis and expand your portfolio. Most self employed professionals try to know everything so they can control and micro-manage their services and business. This has a lot of disadvantages for growth.

Hollywood studio style management of projects where teams assemble on a movie (project) and disband immediately after is employed by most private consulting firms for its cost effectiveness and efficiency. Leverage such a model!

"I like the dreams of the future better than the history of the past"

~ Thomas Jefferson

"You're never too old to set another goal or to dream a new dream"

~ C. S. Lewis

"When you have full belief in yourself and the need to make things happen, that's the powerful force behind being successful"

~ Julia Landauer

Six

ICT:

Visions for the Future

Visions for the Future

Information and communication technology governs almost every aspect of life on earth today. Human life efficiency improvement systems are being developed in large scales and at high rates of production with innovative sense of urgency. It seems science is in a hurry to match the elusive, unfathomable competencies of the creator of the universe.

The progress made so far cannot be credited to technology and science alone. Every knowledge body contributes to the knowledge pool from which scientists, technologists, engineers, and every innovator draws from. What is important for every human in this generation – the information generation – is to key in to technical, emotional and intelligence competencies to thrive. As long as technology continues to evolve with several pervasive digital advancements the world over, technical skills will remain at the forefront of in-demand skills in every industry in the future.

The technologies of the future will be dictated by today's concerns in the combined trends of big data, security, social network and especially automation.

Cast your vision on a future wherein the structures and objects of our physical world are knit together using embedded computation with low-cost sensors and actuators integrated into products we use, locations and even human beings. Healthcare, business, social network and even continuous education would leverage what is known as "ubiquitous sensing" and various location-based tracking systems already in existence for more efficient, automated and highly informed applications. Through these technologies there will be a convergence between the physical world and the virtual world, changing the way we live, manage and track all facets of our personal and professional lives.

The fact is that many of these technologies and systems have already been developed and in use but not yet pervasive or available for end-user applications. Factors like cost, security;

social and cultural limitations as well as innovative intelligence influence their wide adoption on a global scale. Innovative intelligence here refers to the ability to adapt these various existent technologies or products into innovative applications that meet unspecified number of user needs. Sensors or types of sensors for example are found to have more useful applications and adaptations than their initial instance(s) of usage.

Celebrated theorist and philosopher Marshal McLuhan observed that,

"We shape our technologies and thereafter our tools shape us"[1]

His observations capture succinctly, the impact of technology evolution on life and living; and in the future, expect ubiquitous technologies to shape and run our lives, social practices, cultural expectations, and businesses in more unexpected ways than our imaginations can capture.

<u>25</u>

The Internet of Things (IoT)

Many people have heard of the term "Internet of Things" or IoT and it has become a mainstream theme in the technology sector for a while. But what does it mean? As simple as the phrasal connotation is easy to guess literally, do we actually appreciate the impact of its broader implications?

The Global Standards Initiative on Internet of Things (IoT-GSI) defined the IoT as *"a global infrastructure for the information society, enabling advanced services by interconnecting (physical and virtual) things based on existing and evolving interoperable information and communication technologies"*[2].

Today, the internet is strictly seen and evaluated by its inherent capacity to provide humans with interconnectivity solutions; social and business connectivity relative to human-to-human communication. At the center of the systems and the driving force behind information, data, and the communication process from initiation to termination is the human component. But the concept of "internet of things" examines the various existing and emerging physical systems and structures involved and the potentials possible with physical products (objects) around us gaining the capacity to acquire data; exchange data with other connected devices, intelligently analyze same, and respond not just by applying programmed instruction sets but interoperate by intelligently learning from data to make decisions.

This is made possible by embedding electronics, sensors, actuators and software into internet-protocol-enabled (IP-enabled) physical objects; buildings, locations, highways, home appliances, and a variety of other objects as part of the global internet. Any 'thing' that is part of our physical or virtual world which can be integrated into our global communication system as a "connected device" or SMART device will be part of the internet of things.

Summarily, it is not so much something new, but that new and emerging technologies will leverage existing standards, technology infrastructures, technical systems and technologies to extend the level of interconnectedness of people and things, creating a massive unified information system.

What is in it then for the future of aspiring IT professionals? What are the general impact perspectives on the long run?

There is good news and bad news! But the good news far outweighs the bad news. First, the bad news is in the lots of expected job losses especially in other industry sectors to automation and augmented decision systems through artificial intelligence and other technologies. Outdated technical skills within the industry would result to the same impact.

However, the good news is that jobs would be created in more ways and scales than we can imagine. The fact is that there are jobs and activities that cannot remove entirely the involvement of the human component. But the way we do work or what we know today as corporate work may change. Also, new skill areas will be created to match the changing realities of the information age. Let us look at some of the ways the future technologies will impact life and skills – some key directional shifts and some skills and jobs for the future.

Some Future Directional Changes in ICT

In the future, some of the touted technologies already in the works include the following;

Multi-sensory Communication

There are experiments and plans to create products that will aid the absorption of Information through multiple human senses. Today we are experiencing a tremendous flooding of push-notifications from Telcos, applications and other data sources. This multiple information stream sometimes irritates us or throws up a huge challenge processing and analyzing them, especially text-based information.

However, in the nearest future distributed communication channels through human senses will become commonplace for how individuals receive information and businesses evaluate information. By using our sense of smell, touch, sight, taste and sound, information would rather be subtly and intuitively passed on to individuals. This is what the institute for the future predicts would happen. According to their report, *"Advances in psychology and neuroscience are driving new understandings of how the brain processes sensory data."*[3]

While this kind of innovation will reduce information overloads, it may however elicit concerns about invasive manipulation of consumer behaviors and responses, making acceptance varied, they opined. Hopefully, before it becomes widely available, usability tests would have been carried out to address potential conflicts. On the bright side, humans will evolve from having information at hand with distracting flash notifications, to screen-independent communication tools that allow people to fluidly and intuitively merge their digital and physical worlds together.

173

Improved Decision-support

With pervasive big data and analytics using artificial intelligence systems, decision-making will be supported like never before. It is projected that in the next decade critical decisions taken within most organizations will be enhanced by easy access to advanced cloud-based analytical tools which will turn data into useful insights. Analytics which entails linked data, machine intelligence, predictive analytics, computational and virtual simulations, and autonomous algorithms, all utilized to gain massive useful insights from the big data generated today.

Bots (short for internet bot or web robots which are actually software applications used to automate tasks) are already being used in several automation systems, including home automations like smart homes. In the future, several knowledge works will have bots integrated to provide intelligent assistance for various kinds of tasks. The down side is the anticipated job losses and unemployment issues this can create because while there are job domains where analytic and artificial intelligence tools can augment human decision systems, in several cases, they replace them totally. There is hope however to find reprieves for potential job displacements that may occur through social and educational policies.

Information Commercialization

At the rate at which data and information is gaining value as an invaluable asset for organizations, useful, standards-based information will likely be sold, donated and traded in public marketplaces in the near future. As people and organizations understand the true financial, social or other value of their personal data, it will become fashionable to find platforms and marketplaces where they can buy, sell, trade or share their data for personal benefits.

The downside and upside is in the security of data as its value soars, while providing opportunities for security professionals to thrive.

Networked Environments

Imagine a world where nobody is truly alone within an isolated environment, home or enclosure; just about everything biology taught us to regard as inanimate objects are not just active as digital devices but intelligent, exuding seeming emotive behaviors! Components of our environments become conscious, alert to human presence and all connected. Commonplace objects around us that were usually inactive; natural habitats and ecosystems become responsive and knowledgeable.

Imagine a situation where your air-conditioning system senses human presence; and then, adapted to each individual in the house and using acquired, computed bio-data information, it decides the cooling temperature of the room; and when in a group, calculates an average ambient temperature for their aggregate presence. Cool stuff huh?

The Institute for the Future's report sponsored by EMC^2, *The Information Generation: Transforming The Future, Today* summarized it thus,

"As objects become embedded with sensing capacities and connected to the Internet and each other, our environments will become substantially more transparent and responsive. Our homes, and the objects inside them, will fundamentally change as they become networked and connected. For instance, a smart drinking glass could reveal granular nutritional information about its contents, and/or be programmed to track our patterns and anticipate our needs."[4]

Wow! I guess it will throw up a lot of concerns and personal security, privacy and safety issues. My personal belief is that embedded inside challenges are seeds of opportunities too.

Finally, talking about opportunities, let us round up this chapter and book with a list of the ICT specialty areas to watch out for in search of excellence and career progression in the future.

Some Skills and Jobs of the Future
Finally, the following top skill-areas and jobs should provide insight to every professional on what should serve as essential continuing education focus areas in order to remain relevant in the years ahead.
- ✓ *Cloud and distributed computing*
- ✓ *Statistical Analysis and Data Mining*
- ✓ *User Interface Design*
- ✓ *Middleware and Integration Software Skills*
- ✓ *Mobile App development*
- ✓ *Network and Information Security*
- ✓ *Data Analysis and Presentation*
- ✓ Storage Systems and Management
- ✓ *Web architecture and development*
- ✓ *Algorithm design*
- ✓ *Java Development*
- ✓ *SEO/SEM Marketing*

Notes

<u>One</u>

1. Sarah Woodbury, "Messenger Pigeons in the Middle Ages", January 25, 2013. http://www.sarahwoodbury.com/messenger-pigeons-in-the-middle-ages/. Accessed 17 December 2016
2. Wiktionary. See definition, par. 4 "Information". en.wiktionary.org/wiki/information. Accessed 12 November, 2016
3. Stephen B. Wicker, Saejoon Kim (2003). Fundamentals of Codes, Graphs, and Iterative Decoding. Springer. pp. 1 ff. ISBN 1-4020-7264-3.
4. Dusenbery, David B. (1992). Sensory Ecology. W.H. Freeman., New York. ISBN 0-7167-2333-6
5. Barbara Starr, Jeremy Diamond, CNN. 7 April 2017: edition.cnn.com/2017/04/06/politics/donald-trump-syria-military/index.html. Accessed 8 April 2017
6. ITU, International Telecommunications Union. Official website: www.itu.int/en/about/Pages/default.aspx. Accessed 3 March 2017
7. Electronic Industries Alliance. 2011. Archived from the original on 2011-06-02. Retrieved 2011-06-02. The Electronic Industries Alliance ceased operations on February 11, 2011.
8. ISO, International Standards Organization. Official website. www.iso.org/about-us.html. Accessed January 23 2017
9. IEC. Official website. www.iec.ch/about/. Accessed January 23 2017
10. IETF. Official website. www.ietf.org/about/. Accessed January 24 2017
11. Mark, Zuckerberg. Facebook. "Building Jarvis". Monday December 19, 2016.

web.facebook.com/notes/mark-zuckerberg/building-jarvis/10154361492931634/?_rdc=1&_rdr

12. Techcrunch. " Accenture Can I Ask You A Few Questions?". 12 April 2017. techcrunch.com/2017/04/12/accenture-can-i-ask-you-a-few-questions/. Accessed June 20 2017.

13. "Facebook Developer Conference: F8." April 18-19 2017. www.fbf8.com/about. Accessed May 18 2017

14. "The World's Technological Capacity to Store, Communicate, and Compute Information", Martin Hilbert and Priscila López (2011),
Science (journal), 332(6025), 60-65; free access to the article through here:
martinhilbert.net/WorldInfoCapacity.html

15. "World_info_capacity_animation". YouTube. 2011-06-11. Retrieved 2017-05-01.

16. EU_ICT_Professionalism_Project_FINAL_REPORT, "e-SKILLS AND ICT PROFESSIONALISM
Fostering the ICT Profession in Europe", May 2012, pg 14.

TWO

1. IEEE Standard Glossary of Software Engineering Terminology, IEEE std 610.12-1990, 1990.

2. The Assayer (1623), as translated by Thomas Salisbury (1661), p. 178, as quoted in The Metaphysical Foundations of Modern Science (2003) by Edwin Arthur Burtt, p. 75.

3. Deloitte. "ICT Skills Shortage Points to Enormous Opportunities". 16 June 2015. www2.deloitte.com/au/en/pages/media-releases/articles/ict-skills-shortage-points-to-enormous-career-opportunities-160615.html. Accessed January 27 2017

4. EU_ICT_Professionalism_Project_FINAL_REPORT, "e-SKILLS AND ICT PROFESSIONALISM Fostering the ICT Profession in Europe", May 2012

5. EU_ICT_Professionalism_Project_FINAL_REPORT, "e-SKILLS AND ICT PROFESSIONALISM: Fostering the ICT Profession in Europe", May 2012, pg. 25

6. *"e-Skills: Promotion of ICT Professionalism in Europe | No 290/PP/ENT/CIP/13/C/N01C011"*. A report prepared for the European Commission, DG Internal Market, Industry, Entrepreneurship and SMEs, pg. 12

7. SWEBOK. Official website. www.computer.org/web/swebok

8. Nieuwdorp, E. (2007). "The pervasive discourse". *Computers in Entertainment*. **5** (2): 13. doi:10.1145/1279540.1279553

9. "The ICT Profession Body of Knowledge", Professional Standards Board of Australian Computer Society July 2012, pg. 14. Adapted from: Gregor, S., von Konsky, B.R., Hart, R., and Wilson, D. (2008). *The ICT Profession and the ICT Body of Knowledge (Version 5.0)*, Australian Computer Society, Sydney, Australia

10. "The ICT Profession Body of Knowledge", Professional Standards Board of Australian Computer Society July 2012, pg. 14. Adapted from: Gregor, S., von Konsky, B.R., Hart, R., and Wilson, D. (2008). *The ICT Profession and the ICT Body of Knowledge (Version 5.0)*, Australian Computer Society, Sydney, Australia

11. "The ICT Profession Body of Knowledge", Professional Standards Board of Australian Computer Society July 2012, pg. 19. Adapted from: Gregor, S., von Konsky, B.R., Hart, R., and Wilson, D. (2008). *The ICT Profession and the ICT Body of Knowledge (Version 5.0)*, Australian Computer Society, Sydney, Australia

12. Peter Drucker, *Innovation and Entrepreneurship* (New York: Harper Collins, 1993)
13. Peter Drucker, *Innovation and Entrepreneurship* (New York: Harper Collins, 1993)
14. Bill Gates, *Business @ The Speed of Thought: Using a Digital Nervous System* (New York: Warner Books 1999): pg 161-174
15. Steve H. Haeckel and Richard L. Nolan, *1996, Managing by Wire: Using IT to Transform a Business.*
16. Wiktionary. "Operation". See definition en.wiktionary.org/wiki/operation
17. Thomas T. Hewett et al., 1992, Association for Computing Machinery (ACM).
18. Wiktionary. "Resource". See definition en.wiktionary.org/wiki/resource
19. Daniel Goleman, *Working With Emotional Intelligence* (New York 1998): pg 36

THREE

1. Wiktionary. "Consult". See definition en.witionary.org/wiki/consult
2. Stuart Rance and Ashley Hanna (30 May 2007). "Glossary of Terms, Definitions and Acronyms": ITIL – IT Service Management. Office of Government Commerce. Accessed 3 June 2012. en.wikipedia.org/wiki/Service_provider#cite_note-1
3. Bill Gates, *Business @ The Speed of Thought: Using a Digital Nervous System* (New York: Warner Books 1999): pg 134
4. AT&T. "About". Official website. www.att.com/
5. Apple inc. "Apple Financial Statements". fortune.com/global500/list/filtered?sector=Technology. Fortune Global 500. Apple Financial Statements:

www.google.com/finance?q=NASDAQ%3AAAPL&fst
ype=ii&ei=PmqTV9HqNcOeuAS5zpTYBQ.

6. Apple inc. "Company Information". Wikipedia website. en.wikipedia.org/wiki/Apple_Inc. Accessed 12 October 2016

7. Cisco inc. "Cisco Umbrella". Official website. umbrella.cisco.com/.

8. Cisco inc. "Overview". Official website. newsroom.cisco.com/overview. Accessed 22 January 2017

9. Google. Official website, Accessed 12 February 2017. www.google.com/intl/en/about/

10. Google. "About". Official website. Accessed 22 January 2017. www.google.com/intl/en/about/

11. Google. "Company information". Wikipedia website en.wikipedia.org/wiki/Google. Accessed 23 March 2017

12. IBM. "Annual Report". Official website. www.ibm.com/annualreport/2016/images/downloads/IBM-Annual-Report-2016.pdf

13. IBM. "Press release". www-03.ibm.com/press/us/en/presskit/42874.wss. 16 June 2017

14. IBM. "About the company". Accessed 12 February 2017 en.wikipedia.org/wiki/IBM#cite_note-patents-5

15. Citrix, information about the company retrieved 14 February 2017: https://www.citrix.com/about/

16. Strasser, S. (1985) Understanding and Explanation Basic Ideas Concerning the Humanity of the Human Sciences, Duquesne University Press. Pg. 57

17. Skills for the Information Age. https://www.sfia-online.org/en/reference-guide

18. "The ICT Profession Body of Knowledge", Professional Standards Board of Australian Computer Society July 2012, pg. 11. Adapted from: Gregor, S., von Konsky, B.R., Hart, R., and Wilson, D. (2008). *The ICT*

Profession and the ICT Body of Knowledge (Version 5.0), Australian Computer Society, Sydney, Australia

<u>FOUR</u>

1. John Hales. "15 Top-Paying Certifications for 2017". Global knowledge. www.globalknowledge.com/us-en/content/articles/top-paying-certifications/. Accessed 2 June 2017
2. ITIL is now owned by AXELOS. Information about ITIL is sourced from AXELOS official website at: www.axelos.com/certifications/itil-certifications.aspx
3. *COBIT 5,* released by ISACA, Accessed 17 December, 2016. www.isaca.org/COBIT/Pages/Information-Security-Product-Page.aspx
4. CMMI. CMMI official website. cmmiinstitute.com/
5. Prince2. "Prince2 Methods" www.ogc.gov.uk/methods_prince_2.asp (old). AXELOS. www.axelos.com/best-practice-solutions/prince2
6. Jill R Aitoro. "The Basics IT Security Essential Body of Knowledge". www.govexec.com/basics/itsecurity.htm
7. PMI. "Certifications". Official website. www.pmi.org/certifications
8. EC-Council "Programs". Official website. www.eccouncil.org/programs/
9. CompTIA. "Certifications page". official website
10. ISACA, certification information sourced from www.isaca.org/CERTIFICATION/Pages/default.aspx
11. SAS. Official website, Accessed June 13 2017 www.sas.com/en_ph/training/home/get-certified/certification.html
12. The Open Group. "Certifications". Official website. www.opengroup.org/certifications

13. SNIA. Storage Networking Industry Association. "Certifications". Official website. Accessed June 12 2017. www.snia.org/education/certification
14. The SANS Institute. www.sans.org/
15. GIAC. "GIAC Certifications". Official website. www.giac.org/certifications/get-certified/roadmap
16. Check Point. "Certifications". Official website. www.checkpoint.com/ products-solutions/
17. Check Point. "Support services". www.checkpoint.com/support-services/training-certification/
18. Microsoft. "Certifications". Official website. www.microsoft.com/en-us/learning/certification-overview.aspx
19. Oracle "certifications". Oracle official website. education.oracle.com/certification.html
20. Cisco inc. "Certifications". Official website. www.cisco.com/c/en/us/training-events/training-certifications/certifications.html
21. Juniper Networks Certification Program (JNCP), Accessed from official Juniper Networks website. www.juniper.net/us/en/training/certification/. Retrieved 20 April 2017
22. HPE. "Certifications". Official website. learning.hpe.com/tr/certifications
23. *Citrix*, "About the company". Citrix official website, Accessed 11 February 2017.
24. *Citrix,* Citrix website, Accessed 11 February 2017: www.citrix.com/news/announcements/may-2016/citrix-and-microsoft-align-to-help-businesses-embrace-digital-tr.html
25. John Hales. "15 Top-Paying Certifications for 2017". Global knowledge. www.globalknowledge.com/us-en/content/articles/top-paying-certifications/. Accessed 2 June 2017

26. Amazon Web Services. "Certifications". Official AWS website.
27. *VMware*, Accessed 12 July 2017. VMware: https://en.wikipedia.org/wiki/VMwarehttps://www.globa lknowledge.com/us-en/content/articles/top-paying-certifications/
28. *SAP*. SAP official website
29. *SAP*. "Certifications". SAP official website www.sap.com/training-certification/certificate.html
30. *EMC²*, official website. Accessed 2 January, 2017.
31. Dell EMC merger, Wall street Journal report. https://www.wsj.com/articles/dell-closes-60-billion-merger-with-emc-1473252540. Retrieved 2 January, 2017.
32. *Informatica*, Informatica website, Accessed 1 July 2017, "Salesforce Ventures and Microsoft Join Informatica Buyout". nytimes.com. Accessed Aug 7, 2015.
33. *Cloudera*, Cloudera official website, Accessed 4 July 2017. www.cloudera.com/more/news-and-blogs/press-releases/2014-10-20-cloudera-selects-microsoft-azure-as-a-preferred-cloud-platform.html.
34. *Pearson VUE*, https://home.pearsonvue.com/About-Pearson-VUE/What-we-do.aspxSame. Accessed 4 July 2017.
35. Pearson-VUE. "About". Official website. home.pearsonvue.com/About-Pearson-VUE/What-we-do.aspx

FIVE

1. Chukky Oparandu, *"Mobile Phones and Tablets Repairs: A Complete Guide for Beginners and Professionals"* (SC: Mondraim Books, 2016)
2. Daniel Goleman, *Working With Emotional Intelligence* (New York 1998)

3. Joseph Jaworski: quoted in Allen M. Webber, "Destiny and the Job of a Leader", Fast Company, June/July 1996.

SIX

1. Marshal McLuhan, 2016, "Understanding Media: The Extensions of Man".
2. The Global Standards Initiative on Internet of Things (IoT-GSI), 2015. www.itu.int/en/ITU-T/gsi/iot/Pages/default.aspx
3. The Institute For The Future (ITFT), "The Information Generation Transforming the Future, Today: Outlook Report"
4. The Institute For The Future (ITFT), "The Information Generation Transforming the Future, Today: Outlook Report"

Index

Index

Index

Index

Index

W

Also Authored by Chukky Oparandu,

Learn how to fix all kinds of smartphones, tablets, and other microelectronic mobile and hand-held devices!
Visit Amazon marketplaces, eBay, Barnes and Noble and other retail outlets.

About the Author

CHUKKY OPARANDU,

MSc.(ICT), B.Engr.(Electrical/Computer Engineering, F.U.T Minna) is an IT consultant with multi-vendor IT credentials including CCNA, CCNP, OCA. For a decade and half he has been in practice, traversing the field of engineering and information technology implementing myriads of solutions with a variety of vendors' technologies. He has taught, coached and mentored thousands of individuals and corporate personnel through his businesses, government and non-governmental organizations on multiple IT skills and engineering technology. His previous book, *Mobile Phones and Tablets Repairs: A Complete Guide for Beginners and Professionals* is enjoying five star reviews on Amazon with millions sold worldwide.

Contact Chukky through mondraim@gmail.com